I0065221

Starving Billionaires

The History of Inflation and HyperInflation

TABLE OF CONTENTS

DISCLAIMER

Copyright © 2021

All Rights Reserved

No part of this eBook can be transmitted or reproduced in any form, including print, electronic, photocopying, scanning, mechanical, or recording, without prior written permission from the author.

While the author has taken the utmost effort to ensure the accuracy of the written content, all readers are advised to follow the information mentioned herein at their own risk. The author cannot be held responsible for any personal or commercial damage caused by the information. All readers are encouraged to seek professional advice when needed.

Introduction

Introduction

Imagine a loaf of bread doubling in a matter of hours. Despite being extreme, this becomes the reality of hyperinflation, where prices rise exponentially, and money becomes worthless. Inflation has become a prominent subject of discussion in the United States and across the world. Despite current concerns regarding the impact of a devalued dollar on the economy, history reveals how past inflations have been much worse than today. In 2008, Steve Hanke, a professor at Johns Hopkins University, researched the Zimbabwean hyperinflation to see how it compared to historical instances of the same (Toscano, 2014). The study revealed that hyperinflation typically coincides with wars and a set of ill-advised and uninformed fiscal policies. However, the primary cause is a quick increase in the money supply without economic growth. The first recorded hyperinflation in modern times occurred during the French Revolution, where monthly inflation rose to

143% (Tosnano, 2014). This kind of inflation only appeared again in the 20th century.

This book discusses several great inflations and hyperinflations throughout the history of civilizations, from Ancient Rome to the current problems in Venezuela. In the 20th century, seventeen hyperinflations occurred in Europe and Central Asia, including five in Latin America, four in Western Europe, one in Asia, and one in Africa. A look at the United States reveals that the country had never experienced hyperinflation but came close twice during the Revolutionary War and the Civil War when the national government printed money to cater to its war initiatives. Nonetheless, in the American cases, inflation never surpassed a 50% monthly rate, which is significantly lower than history`s hysterics cases.

Scholars assert that hyperinflations had never happened when commodity acted as money or when paper currency converts to a hard asset. Hyperinflation mainly occurs when the money supply had no natural constraints and was controlled by a discretionary paper money standard. Although hyperinflation mandates a series of extreme political and social events, we see that fiat currency is vulnerable to rampant inflation. The economic costs of hyperinflation include a fall in the value of savings, unemployment, lack of confidence in the finance sector, and lack of investment and economic growth.

The most devastating hyperinflation happened in Hungary in July 1946, when prices surged by 4.19 quintillion percent. Another severe hyperinflation was in Germany from 1922 to 1923, when prices doubled every two days. The most recent hyperinflation episode is happening in Venezuela since 2016 (Toscano, 2014). This book looks at ten different hyperinflations across history, starting with the fall of Ancient Rome and ending in the Venezuelan disaster.

What are Inflation and Hyperinflation?

Inflation is a sustained increase in the aggregate price level; and measures the growth rate in prices for a diversified range of products and services. It is the decline of purchasing power of a particular currency over time. The first thing to comprehend regarding hyperinflation is that it is not just high inflation. High inflation refers to the general rise in prices and wages. High inflation is very disruptive. For instance, during the 1970s, the UK point prices rose by more than 20% annually, ushering in a decade of civil unrest and financial turmoil (Amadeo, 2020).

Hyperinflation is a completely different ball game. Hyperinflation occurs when prices rise at a rate of more than 50% per month (Amadeo, 2020). At this rate, an item worth $1 in January would cost at least $130 at the end of the year. It means that a loaf of bread would cost higher in the afternoon than in the morning. It represents the point at which faith in a nation`s currency and economy are dead. As a result, the currency is effectively worthless. Hyperinflation is widely a 20th-century phenomenon. The most explored hyperinflation happened in Germany after World War I when the country experienced a monthly inflation rate of 322% (Salemi, 2021). On average, prices quadrupled every month during the sixteen months of hyperinflation.

What causes hyperinflation? No single shock, no matter how devastating, can explain sustained, consistent, quick growth of prices. The two world wars did not cause hyperinflation in Germany and

Hungary. Hyperinflation has two primary causes: increased money supply and demand-pull inflation (Salemi, 2021). An increase in money supply happens when the monetary and fiscal authorities start printing money to pay for a large stream of government expenditures. As the money supply increases, so do the prices.

On the other hand, demand-pull inflations occur when a surge in demand surpasses supply, sending prices up. This scenario occurs when consumer spending increases because of a growing economy, an instant rise in exports, or increased government spending. The two factors go hand-in-hand. Rather than restricting the money supply to reduce inflation, the state continues to print more money. Consequently, prices surge since there is too much money circulating. Here, the consumers expect inflation to continue rising; thus, they purchase more in the present to avoid paying a greater price in the future. Excessive demand worsens inflation.

What are the effects of hyperinflation?

One of the primary effects of hyperinflation is the relocation of wealth. Hyperinflations transfer wealth from the public, which holds money, to the state, which issues money. It leads to shortages as individuals begin to hoard both durable and perishable goods. As a result, daily commodities become scarce, and the economy crashes. Additionally, life savings become worthless, and financial institutions collapse as their loans lose value and people stop making deposits.

Hyperinflation severely diminishes the value of a currency in foreign exchange markets, making it hard for importers to buy foreign commodities. Unemployment rises as businesses close and government tax revenue declines. In most cases, the state prints more money as a response to pay its bills, worsening the hyperinflation. However, there are two primary winners in hyperinflation. Those who have loans benefit as the higher prices make their debt worthless. Exporters win big since their exports are cheaper than foreign competitors.

Venezuelan Hyperinflation

The most recent instance of hyperinflation is in Venezuela. The suffering of millions of Venezuelans has been broadcast across the world to demonstrate the raw devastation that hyperinflation can cause. Venezuela used to be one of the richest countries in the world in the 1960's. It had a GDP per capita better than Norway at that time. Failure to diversify their economy away from oil and lackluster governance and embrace of extreme socialist programs has seen a slow decline over the decades, eventually resulting in a modern-day catastrophe.

While the seeds of destruction were sown for decades, the actual trees started growing in the early 2010s. In 2013, prices increased by 41%, and by 2018, inflation was at 65,000%. Between 2014 and 2016, the poverty rate increased from 50% to over 80%. In response to the inflation, the state increased the money supply by 14% in 2017 (Caraballo, Madrid & Barrios, 2018). The people responded by utilizing eggs as currency. In January 2017, a carton of eggs was valued at 6,740 bolivars, and unemployment increase by over 20%. This unemployment was similar to the United States during the Great Depression (Caraballo, Madrid & Barrios, 2018). It got so bad that the populace could no longer afford most essential commodities, as shown in Figure 1.

Figure 1. *The changing Venezuelan diet*

The changing Venezuelan diet

As food prices skyrocket...	...Venezuelans can no longer afford many staples
Year-on-year price increase of food and non-alcoholic beverages (%)	Share of families who said they buy each product (%)

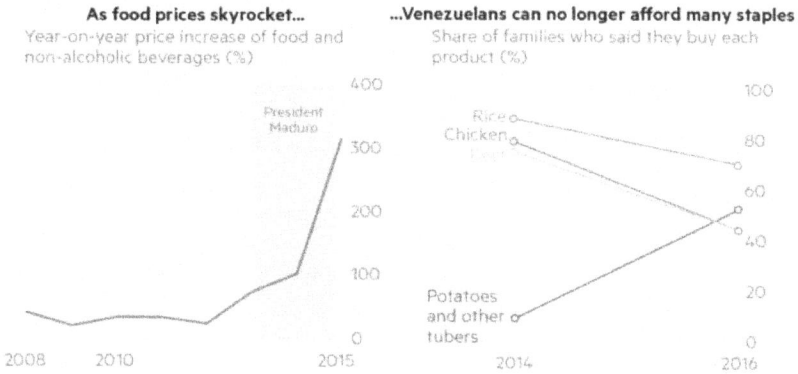

Source: (Population Pyramid, 2019)

What caused the hyperinflation?

Former President Hugo Chavez had implemented price regulations for essential commodities such as food and medicine. However, these prices were low and mandated domestic firms to close shop. In reaction, the state paid for imports. In 2016, oil prices declined drastically, eroding revenue from state-run oil firms.

Consequently, the government went broke and began printing more currency. By 2019, the country's foreign debt had accumulated to around $100 billion, and in 2020, the yearly inflation rate for consumer price was about 150,000% (Multimore, 2021). Currently, the Venezuelan government is promoting a new cryptocurrency to offset inflation since the Bolivar has lost most of its value against

11

international currencies. The country cannot afford to continue printing money. As the nation's economy continues to collapse, the country faces an enormous debt repayment problem. The exchange rate has been skyrocketing since 2015, as shown in Figure 2 below. Today, Venezuela is the only nation on the planet suffering from hyperinflation.

Figure 2. *Money Supply, exchange rate, and consumer prices.*

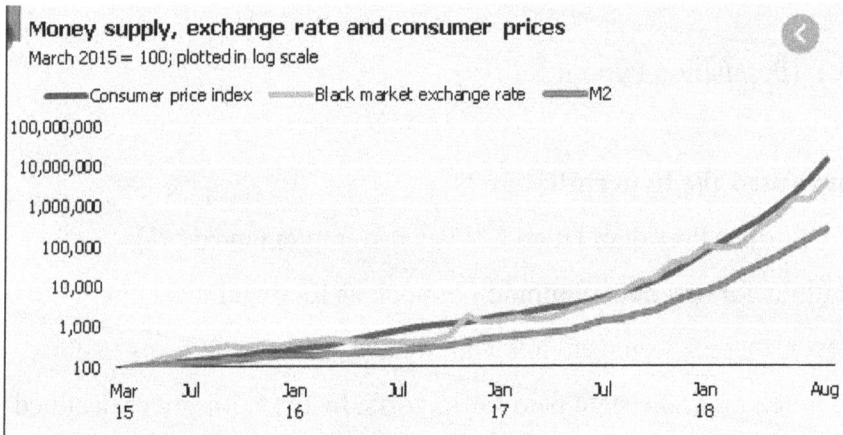

Money supply, exchange rate and consumer prices
March 2015 = 100; plotted in log scale

Consumer price index — Black market exchange rate — M2

Source: (Venezuela Money Supply, 2021)

The Lead Up to Hyperinflation

To understand Venezuela's path to hyperinflation, it is essential to analyze the country's economic, social, and political environment.

The collapse of the economy, the scarcity of essential goods and services, and public transportation.

First, we look at Venezuela's natural resource 'curse' to understand the recurrent hyperinflation. The nation is an excellent example of an oil-reliant economy that failed with its trade policy since it is heavily dependent on its oil deposits as a trading product. Venezuela's oil economy started in 1914 when the Caribbean Oil Company discovered substantial oil reserves (Koech, 2016). Soon, the nation began exporting oil, and the commodity quickly became Venezuela's primary export. Today, the oil reserves are estimated to be around 38,291 billion barrels and are the largest oil deposits in the world (Koech, 2016). Its primary trading partners are the US, China, and Russia. However, the relationship between Venezuela and the US is strained ever since President Maduro accused the US of plotting to overthrow his administration and undermine Venezuela's economy. The US imposed sanctions against Venezuela between 2014 and 2018. They imposed a ban on using oil from Venezuela, which greatly damaged the economy. Venezuela now has limited customers for its large oil reserves. China is the second-largest oil trading partner of Venezuela.

Venezuela's oil exports account for approximately 96% of its total exports, which is about 30% of its GDP (Koech, 2016). The second global oil crisis took place in 1980, ignited by the first Gulf War. As a result, the Bolivar depreciated drastically, and commodities within Venezuela become more expensive. For instance, benzene prices shot up, and public transport tickets increased in price (Koech, 2016). Consequently, in 1989, a significant part of the population demonstrated, leading to regulations that made Benzene cheaper than water.

Venezuela's heavy dependence on an oil economy has caused other sectors to suffer enormously since the 1940s. Subsequent socialist governments have concentrated their trade approaches on the export of oil and neglected other sectors. This made Venezuela's imports cheaper and helped the Bolivar become a strong currency in the global economy. Consequently, foreign nations couldn't afford local commodities from Venezuela, and the nation's agricultural sector collapsed, destroying the livelihood of most Venezuelan individuals. The nation's food production system is now completely based on socialism and food rations.

Another factor that is significant to Venezuela's path to hyperinflation is its weak corporate governance. The era of socialism started in 1998 when President Hugo Chavez was elected. Under his administration, the nation's name was changed to the Bolivarian Republic of Venezuela (Pittaluga, Seghezza & Morelli, 2021). The president announced that every citizen would benefit from the country's rich oil deposits. Chavez's administration enjoyed a lucky era, as oil prices surged five-fold during his tenure. At the start of Chavez's tenure, oil prices were at the lowest in the nation's history, and at his death, the price had increased ten times. The increased oil revenues enabled the state to invest in social initiatives, such as healthcare and housing, and reduce poverty and inequality.

However, the government failed to invest in other economic sectors believing that the rich oil deposits could sustain the nation's economy. Similarly, the state expected oil prices to remain stable. The state subsidized gas prices, which led to smuggling. The state, however, failed to take action and stop this smuggling, weakening the nation's actual output. Despite Chavez increasing the price of gas, the country still has the cheapest gas prices in the world (Pittaluga, Seghezza & Morelli, 2021). This was the onset of inflation. The cost of goods and services then began to increase within the country, causing high inflation. From then, the value of the Bolivar continued to decline, prompting the government to introduce a fixed dollar exchange rate in an attempt to stabilize the currency. However, this effort proved futile since the Bolivar's value was much less than the state wanted to admit.

Another factor that paved the way for Venezuela's hyperinflation was the exploitation of private companies. The country nationalized the oil sector in the 1970s, and these corporations controlled the industry and embarked on business with foreign firms (Pittaluga, Seghezza & Morelli, 2021). However, when Chavez became president, he decided to place political appointees as heads of these

15

public companies to control them. Most of the appointed executives had no experience or knowledge in the oil sector, leading to badly run oil companies and significant corruption. As a result, oil workers went on a two-month strike, crippling the oil sector nationally. The government responded by firing more than 18,000 employees, and in the following years, more companies were nationalized. For instance, in 2007, Exxon was forced to hand over its shares to the governments. Between 1998 and 2013, Venezuela`s oil profits increased by 90% (Pittaluga, Seghezza & Morelli, 2021).

By the time the Chavez regime was over, Venezuela was a completely government-controlled state, including the steel, power, and food industries. These economic actions eliminated the foundation of a free economy as the state heavily regulated the job market, prohibiting companies from dismissing workers in crises. When President Nicolas Maduro entered office, his administration continued the ongoing nationalization of private firms, causing many companies to go bankrupt. Additionally, the oil prices fell from $111 per barrel in 2013 to $57.60 in 2014. A year later, the oil prices fell to $37.60, and in 2016, the prices ranged between $27.10 and $57.69 (Pittaluga, Seghezza & Morelli, 2021).

Figure 3. *Oil production reduction*

Oil production is falling

Millions of barrels per day

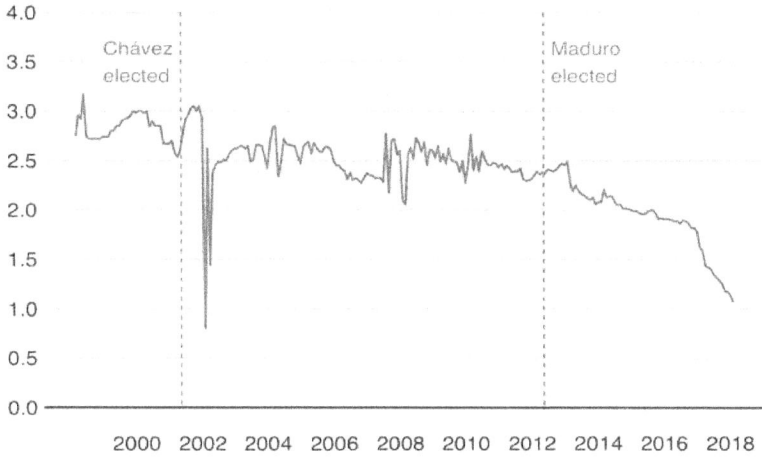

Source: (Trading Economics, 2021).

    As a result, the Venezuelan economy declined by 30% from 2013 to 2017, and the dependence on food and consumer goods imports increased immensely. The shrinking economy caused the foreign debt to decrease from $30 billion in 2013 to less than $10 billion in 2018, as shown in the figure. Also, the Trump administration imposed sanctions on the country, forcing the government to print more money.

First Signs of Hyperinflation

Experts stipulate that Venezuela's economy started to witness hyperinflation during the first year of President Maduro's regime. The probable causes of hyperinflation include printing more currency and deficit spending. When Maduro took over in 2013, the annual inflation rate was around 30%, and by 2014, it had increased to 61.5%. However, the government did not release the nation's statistics in an attempt to manipulate public perception. Figure 4 clearly shows the extent of inflation under Maduro. Many international and local agencies, such as the IMF, stipulated that numerous loose macroeconomic policies had created high inflation in Venezuela and drained its foreign reserves. Some experts state that the inflation was around 300% in March 2014 as opposed to the official inflation rate of 60%. In September and October 2014, the Venezuelan government failed to release inflation data.

Also, Venezuelans did not believe that their nation was facing high inflation since there was a lot of money circulating in the economy and few shortages. In 2014, the supply of Bolivar increased by 64%, three times quicker than any other nation in the world.

Figure 4. *Venezuela's Inflation after Maduro's Election.*

Venezuela's inflation spiked after Maduro's election

Estimate for 2018 is off the scale

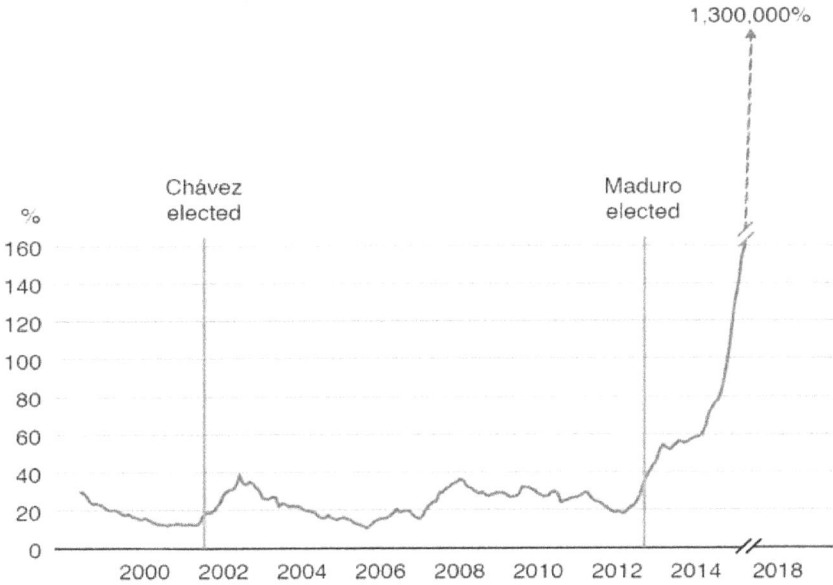

Source: (Trading Economics, 2021).

Maduro`s administration blamed capitalist speculation for hyperinflation and creating widespread shortages of essential goods and services. The state focused on fighting an economic war by implementing new financial measures against political opponents. However, these initiatives were more strategies that tried to hide the extent of the nation`s high inflation. Today, Maduro is criticized for focusing on public opinion rather than addressing real issues regarding hyperinflation.

Hyperinflation Years

As it stands today, Venezuela is close to running out of foreign exchange reserves, and it has lost access to overseas debt markets. Venezuela has also lost support of other governments because of political corruption and its nationalization of multinationals.

The Venezuelan economy declined by 5.8% in the first quarter of 2010, with an inflation rate of 30.5% (Koech, 2016). However, by the time Chavez died in 2013, Venezuela had entered a recession. Consumer prices increased exponentially during this time. By 2010, inflation had reversed any progress in wage increases. Venezuela officially entered hyperinflation in November 2016 after inflation passed the 50% mark. According to the IMF, the country experienced a 500% inflation rate in 2016 since the monthly inflation surpassed 50% for the 30th consecutive day (Koech, 2016).

In 2017, the inflation rate reached 4,000%. Consequently, the citizens started a trend of gold farming in cyber games to attain hard currency. During the Christmas season in 2017, most stores did not use price tags due to inflation. According to the Venezuelan government, the inflation rate was 274% in 2017, 863% in 2018, and 130,060% in 2019 (Koech, 2016). However, according to IMF, the inflation rate was 929, 790% in 2018, and over 10,000,000% in 2019 (Koech, 2016).

In 2016, the Bolivar witnessed its largest-ever loss of value. In November, the exchange rate reached 2,000 Bolivar for one USD, and by the 28th of the same month, the currency had lost 60% of its value to reach 3,000 Bolivar per USD (Multimore, 2021). As a result, the state retired the subsidized 10 Bolivar per USD exchange rate in January 2018, making the currency the second least-valued currency in circulation in the world.

Additionally, the minimum wage in the country dropped considerably before and during the hyperinflation period. Between 2012 and 2015, the minimum wage declined from around $360 per month to approximately $31. Following the release of a new currency in 2018, the minimum wage increased from 392,646 Bolivar to 180 million Bolivar per month. In terms of USD, the minimum monthly salary was equivalent to $5 by the end of April 2020 (Multimore, 2021).

During the hyperinflation era, unemployment increased drastically in Venezuela. In 2019, the unemployment rate rose to unprecedented levels; levels not seen since the end of the Bosnia War in 1995. In January 2016, the unemployment rate was 18.1%, and by October 2019, it had reached 35%. By 2020, the rate had increased to 40%, causing many individuals to immigrate to other nations. According to UNHCR, emigration from Venezuela during 2015 is regarded as one of the biggest emigrations in modern history as more than 4.8 million Venezuelans have registered as refugees and migrants (Caraballo, Madrid & Barrios, 2018).

Impact on Individuals

As Venezuela battles inflation, barter and dollars became the new reality. Citizens have been forced to find alternative ways to pay for essential products and services. During hyperinflation, people carry lots of cash around. A shocking example is shown in Figure 4, where the price of a chicken is to the tune of 14m bolivars. However, in Venezuela, the capacity to get hard money has declined significantly. Bolivar notes are increasingly scarce since the government mint no longer works. As a result, the country must source banknotes from abroad. Today, Venezuelans use barter, dollars, and other alternative payment systems since one can go for weeks without touching banknotes (Koech, 2016).

Figure 4. *Money needed to purchase a chicken (14m Bolivars).*

Source: (Partington, 2018)

The Deleveraging

Since the hyperinflation, the Venezuelan government has embarked on several initiatives to tackle inflation and reduce its debts. Despite these measures, Venezuela is still experiencing hyperinflation in 2021. Following the start of the hyperinflation, the state introduced higher denomination banknotes. In December 2016, new notes with higher denominations including 500, 1000, 5000, 10000, and 20000 Bolivars were issued since the 100 Bolivar note was only worth $0.23. In March 2021, the state introduced three new notes to the public, including 200000, 500000, and 100000 Bolivar notes, with the latest note being worth $0.52 (Huertas, 2019).

Moreover, the government introduced the Petro cryptocurrency in 2017 to try and stabilize the economy. The new cryptocurrency is backed by the nation`s oil, gold, and diamond reserves (Huertas, 2019). Although the cryptocurrency promised to mitigate some of the economic challenges, it has not gathered momentum in Venezuela and the international community.

From the start of 2019, the government embarked on controlling inflation via a combination of fiscal, monetary, and exchange rate policies. Expenditures reduced, VAT increased, bank reserve ratios increased, and the central bank got rid of several regulations on access to foreign currency (Huertas, 2019). Due to increased sanctions in 2019, the state abandoned protectionist policies like price and currency controls, liberating the economy. The extents of these spending cuts are difficult to approximate since most of the information is not released to the public. However, some reports suggest that government expenditures have decreased considerably. Since then, Venezuela has seen its economy rebound from the recession. The fiscal consolidation has yielded some results as hyperinflation fell by close to 200% in 2019 and 2020 (Huertas, 2019).

The state has also modified the exchange rate to offset the crisis. Between August and September 2018, the state temporarily lifted currency controls, allowing individuals and companies to buy and sell foreign exchange (Huertas, 2019). The state also unified and devalued the exchange and announced a new currency that matched the informal price, limiting the black market. In August 2018, the government introduced the Bolivar Soberano with one Bolivar Soberano worth 100,000 Bolivar (Huertas, 2019). The new Bolivar was devalued by close to 96% compared to the old Bolivar against the USD, as shown in Figure 5.

Figure 5.

Official and black market exchange rates in Venezuela, November 2018–June 2019

bolívares per US dollar

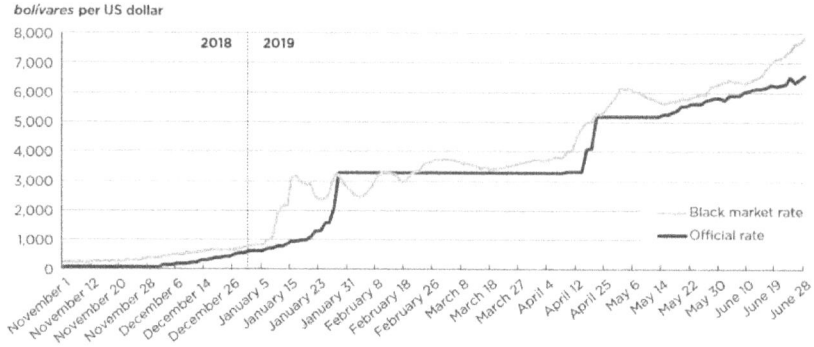

Source: (Hyperinflation in Venezuela: A Stabilization Handbook, 2019).

The introduction of the new currency did not stop inflation. It increased from 48,750% to 65,000% by the end of the month (Huertas, 2019). In January 2019, the state introduced a fixed exchange rate, but by 2020, it has given up on the exchange rate and embraced more of a free-floating exchange rate.

US Revolutionary War Great Inflation

Like many other nations, the United States started as a colony and had to fight for its independence. From 1775 to 1783, the country fought an all-out war with its colonial master Great Britain. This became known as the US revolutionary war since it changed the region's history. Following the war, economic turmoil and inflation hit the nation, leading to financial hardships. It was the foundation of the American civil war entailing infighting among American citizens. Now, let us look into the revolutionary war period, emphasizing its implications on the country's economic downturn. The chapter articulates events leading up to the war and the consequent significant inflation that hit the United States. It also investigates elements surrounding the inflation years and how ordinary citizens fared during this period. Also discussed in the chapter are the efforts taken by the leaders to salvage the situation with economic policies used to stir up growth taking center stage. The US revolutionary war is a viable example of the role of war in destabilizing the economy and disrupting currency circulation.

The Leadup to the Great Inflation

Towards the second half of the 18th century, Great Britain continued to reign supreme over other nations, taking up colonies in nearly all continents around the globe. Its far-reaching power had considerable implications on its territories and their economic capabilities. Following the French and Indian wars, also known as the Seven Year Wars, Great Britain had drained its revenue and ability to support its vast military. By 1763, when these wars ended, Britain was gasping for an economic revamp and looking for new revenue sources (Bezanson, 2016). Its national debt had skyrocketed, and hence it looked for adopted taxation policies aimed at changing the situation. Maintaining and populating the British troops in the colonies they had conquered was subject to the funds they would obtain from these frontiers. Therefore, they imposed the Stamp and Townshend Acts targeting the British American colonies (Ferraro, 2021). These policies looked to impose direct taxation on the colonies and enforce higher taxation policies. These acts also increased the Britain legislature's power over colonies for tax and control of economic policies.

It is vital to point out that the Townshend and Stamp acts came in between 1767 and 1768. Other policies looking to increase taxation, such as the Sugar Act and Tea Act, also came in the following years. These were not well received in the colonies. They provoked colonial opposition and unrest whereby the British American colonies' inhabitants resisted the heavy taxation (Ferraro, 2021). They claimed that they would not agree to taxation without representation in the British legislature. On March 5th 1770, the Boston massacre was the tipping point of this resistance. An angry mob confronted British soldiers in Boston leading to a massacre (Hamilton, 1977). The Boston tea party followed the Boston massacre in 1773. Patriots and merchants resisted and burnt up a British ship bringing in tax free tea from China. Great Britain responded by instilling punitive measures known as the Intolerable Acts of 1774 (Taskinsoy, 2020). These policies were meant to punish the colony for the Boston tea party and resistance towards the

Tea acts. In response, Americans took up arms, and an all-out battle broke out in 1775 led by George Washington.

Figure 1. *The Boston tea party 1773*

Source: (Hamilton, 1977)

The American War of Independence marked the start of events that led to an inflationary period like no other. To get into war with Great Britain meant that the United States had to amass significant resources for the campaign. One of the most critical elements in this war would be financing to recruit and pay soldiers. It is crucial to indicate that Americans were highly opposed to taxation. Therefore, the leaders opted to raise revenue through means other than tax. They printed more currency to increase monetary circulation, and laws were put in place to ensure people exchanged goods and services in paper currency or specie (Bredin & Fountas, 2018). The increase in the circulation of the continental dollar was vital in increasing the revenue available for military spending.

The American leaders also opted to print bills of credit redeemable for future taxes. The continental congress was digging a pit that would later lead the United States into economic turmoil. The country suffered inflation at the expense of independence, and it took decades to recover from this predicament fully.

Figure 2. *American Revolutionary War*

Source: (Bredin & Fountas, 2018)

The First Signs

The first signs of inflation showed when the young republic struggled to develop economic freedom. Having cut ties with its primary trade partner and provider of manufactured goods, the United States had to restructure its economic policies to augment its liberty (Ferraro, 2021).

It is crucial to point out that Britain had also barred the United States from trading with the sugar colonies in the Caribbean, leaving the region to develop internal trade. Additionally, Britain's naval force blockaded all trade routes and left the United States to fend for itself. With the situation at hand, the country had to deal with a looming economic crisis. They had to discover new ways to generate revenue, given that taxation was not possible. It struggled to settle the debts incurred while the continental dollar lost value in favor of silver coins (Taskinsoy, 2020). There was excessive currency in circulation, leading to an exponential increase in the price of goods and services.

Figure 3. *Continental currency printed to support the revolutionary*

war

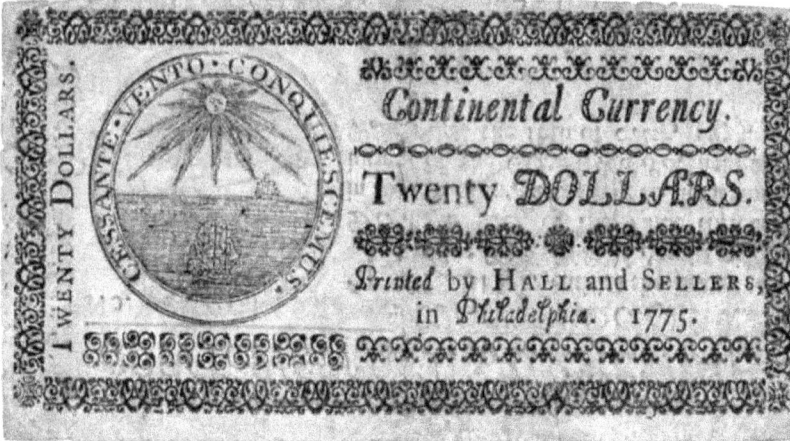

Source: (Bezanson, 2016)

A significant aspect to point out is that every state had the ability to

print continental dollars in addition to the federal government. Thus, the

rates of inflation in each state were different. For example, in Virginia,

hyperinflation kicked in by 1779, with inflation increasing more than

50% monthly (Bezanson, 2016). Other early signs of inflation appeared

when the amount of currency flowing in the region increased despite

shortages in goods and services. It is crucial to note that individuals had hoarded currency earlier during the war, spending little due to uncertainty. However, towards the end of the war, individuals started spending, but there was not much to purchase. There was, therefore, excessive circulation of continental dollars, which in many senses reduced its value. Other early signs included the government's increased spending despite the ever-increasing national debt (Taskinsoy, 2020). Furthermore, inclination towards taxation and price controls to limit the ever-increasing costs of goods indicated that the government had realized that inflation would continue destabilizing the region's economy.

The Inflationary Years

The populace felt most of the inflation after the end of the war. As indicated earlier, the troops incurred much of the expenses, promoting the continental congress to develop ingenious means to increase revenue generation. By 1780, the United States had issued about 400 million dollars to its army. Congress put up a spirited fight to counter the runaway inflation, but its tactics only devalued the continental dollar further. From 1775 there was an average annual inflation rate of 4.5% over the next decade (Hamilton, 1977). The worst year was 1778 when inflation reached an all-time high of 29%. This spelt economic doom for the region, unless the leaders implemented drastic control measures (Hamilton, 1977). This inflation was followed by disloyalty towards the new government, outright resistance, and protests with significant civil unrest. Discontent over rising prices increased rapidly, spreading from state to state, and people started taking up arms to counter the continental congress's agenda. Numerous food riots were the order of the day during this period, with large plantation owners inciting the peasants to hold the government to account for the economic downturn.

Figure 4. *Inflation during and after the American War for*

Independence

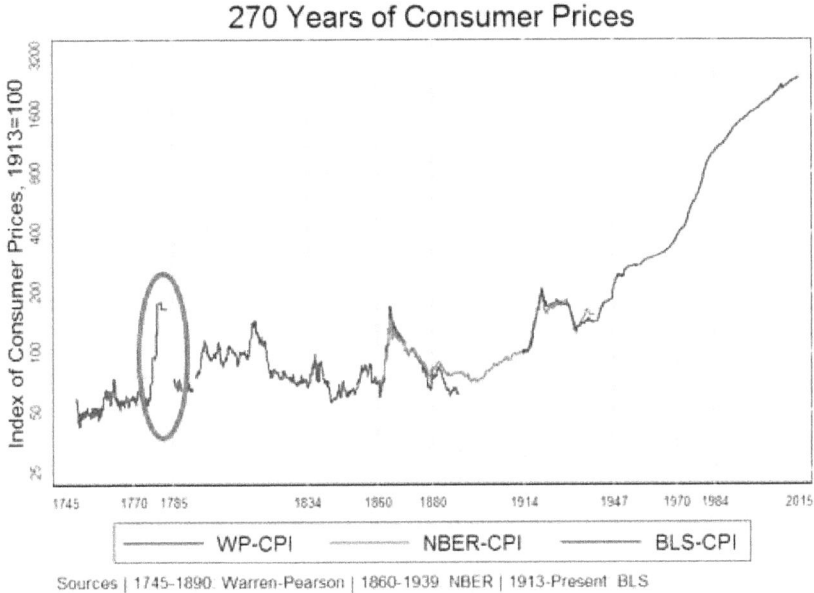

270 Years of Consumer Prices

Sources | 1745-1890 Warren-Pearson | 1860-1939 NBER | 1913-Present BLS

Source: (Hamilton, 1977)

The continental congress responded by printing even more

dollars thereby devaluing the continental dollar. With the devaluation of

the currency came an increase in prices of goods and services, causing

further unease among ordinary citizens. Congress also faced another critical issue with counterfeit continental dollars in circulation. This increased inflation rates significantly and sabotaged the region's economic progress. It was Britain primarily spread the counterfeit currency to derail America's recovery process. Great Britain counted on the counterfeit continental dollars to help them win the war and increase America's dependence on them (Bredin & Fountas, 2018). However, America's road towards independence accelerated with the development of a constitution and the growth of political institutions. The inhabitants held liberty in high regard, and therefore despite economic turmoil, they wanted nothing to do with their former colonizers. In many senses, the hardships experienced during the inflationary years helped shape the United States. The resilience of the United States lasted far beyond this period and is one of the reasons they became a long-term superpower.

The troops played a significant role in increasing inflation during and after the American revolutionary war. Late into the war, the continental congress decided on each state's role in supporting its troops. It is crucial to point out that there was no national or central bank during this period, and therefore monetary control remained elusive (Aizenman & Marion, 2011). In the wake of these policies, the states went overboard in equipping and servicing their troops. To pay for the soldiers' upkeep, the states printed more continental currencies while imposing taxation on their citizens. This further made controlling inflation an uphill task since each state had its own methods, policies, and consequent inflation rates. By the time the war ended, the United States federal government had spent about 37 million dollars while the states had spent about 114 million dollars (Hildebrand, 2018). The states had to negotiate with the continental congress to reduce the money supply and counter inflation in respective regions. These efforts put the young republic in jeopardy, further halting economic progress with runaway inflation. The debts incurred in maintaining troops and the closure of trade routes caused the post-war economic slump.

There was also the flooding of British goods at cheaper prices and increased money supply. This fueled rampant inflation reducing American quality of life and ability to trade. Many traders and merchants preferred barter with increasing debts calling for new means of currency exchange. One such method was the exchange of tobacco for notes redeemable in shops.

Currency debts were issued in the form of currency notes which were to be paid back later (Baack, 2008). These debts eliminated a standard currency value and consequent outright currency power. It led to economic issues that prompted the continental congress to develop policies to loosen laws governing debt repayment. Relaxation of prison terms, repossession, and public shaming were strategies adopted to force those in debt to pay up their dues. This, however, angered the conservatives and those who looked to get paid, further putting the currency system at risk. The inflationary years became a battle between those with and those without, hence forming the Republican and Democrat factions.

Figure 5. *Credit notes*

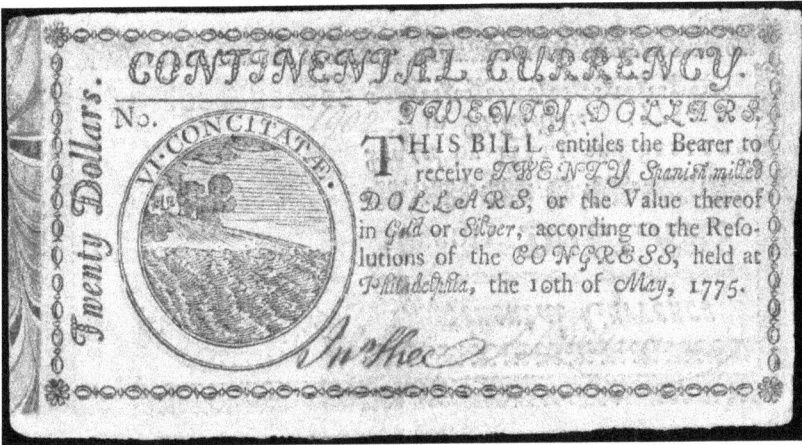

Source: (Baack, 2008)

How the Common Man Fared During the Inflationary Period

During the inflationary period, the citizens had a hard time

surviving the ongoing economic crisis. There was paper money that

continued to become worthless, combined with a lack of quality goods

due to the closure of trade between the US and Great Britain.

Additionally, limited exports meant that many ordinary citizens had

little or no means of livelihood and hence suffered dearly (Hildebrand,

2018).

The Britain loyalists faced it rough due to castigation for supporting Britain. They were attacked and their estates were repossessed by the patriots who felt entitled to their wealth. The soldiers who had participated in the revolutionary war also had a rough time integrating into society. Despite compensation in land, they could only practice subsistence farming for barter trade (Berg, 2021). They, therefore, had limited economic prosperity as earlier promised by the state. They became ordinary citizens who were at the mercy of the government's policies in reversing inflation and increasing the region's economic growth.

It is essential to note that the continental government did not have the powers to impose taxation to generate revenue. It, therefore, continued to print paper money while borrowing domestically. Towards the end of the war, those that lent to the government were paid with obligations to pay (IOU notes) and therefore had minimal revenue to spend (Hildebrand, 2018). Life got harder for ordinary citizens, but it was much worse for the slaves. The slaves that participated in the war with the promise of liberty found themselves back into the shackles of slavery. They did not enjoy the promised freedom and instead continued under their masters as before the war. Women were also disregarded post-war despite their critical role during the war. Equality was out of the equation, and they went back to their role of being housewives (Bredin & Fountas, 2018). These aspects indicate that the common man had a tough life, but this was the situation across the board. All social classes were suffering, and the government had to develop drastic measures to salvage the situation.

Figure 6. *Women during the revolutionary war*

Source: (Bredin & Fountas, 2018).

The government implemented measures to control prices, which did not augur well with ordinary citizens and merchants. Many hoarded goods and were later robbed as the government looked to repossesses their property. Soldiers were also notorious for taking what was not theirs, raiding farmlands, taking grain, wine and animals for their supplies (Hildebrand, 2018). They were bad news to peasant farmers since they saw it as their right to take whatever was in their path to help sustain their ability to fight. Free speech also suffered during this period, given that dissent was strongly squashed. The army procurement officers started seizing whatever supplies were needed and providing certificates of debts in return. They, therefore, oppressed the common man for war.

To make matters worse, they did not allow complaints or grievances. The policy antagonized the ordinary citizens making their lives difficult (Bezanson, 2016). Many hid their horses and dismantled their wagons to keep them away from the soldiers. In other cases, they snuck behind the soldiers' lines to take back what was theirs. Therefore, it is accurate to conclude that the inflationary years caused strife between the common man, the army, and the government.

The Deleveraging

Economic reforms aimed at reducing inflation bore fruits about five decades later after the end of the revolutionary war. The continental congress realized that despite the convenience of the specie, the region needed a paper currency to enhance its economic dominance. They, therefore, continued to issue the continental dollar at a controlled rate while developing policies to limit barter trade. The continental congress also set up the Bank of America as a national reserve to lend loans to the government. According to Berg (2021), it imposed Gresham's law which looked to ensure that the region did away with specie in favor of paper currency. Individuals had hoarded large sums of coin currency flowing in from trade with Havana and the French troops. However, this law ensured that it was eliminated from circulation and used for imports. The United States now had depreciated paper currency as the primary medium of exchange. It imposed taxes, opened up trade, and increased government expenditure to open up the region's economy. Towards 1840, the region's economic growth picked up pace, increasing the dollar's value and balancing money circulation in the economy (Berg, 2021). The United States eventually overcame the inflation and has been on an upward economic trend ever since.

Hyperinflation during the US Civil War

The southern states experience a classic case of hyperinflation during the US Civil War (1861-1865). When the war ended, the confederate currency was worthless. The North also faced significant financial hardship but had a thriving economy centered on railroads and factories. The South was solely dependent on farming, and the abolition of slave labor brought the entire economy to its knees.

The tension between the Northern and Southern states had been brewing years earlier. Slave labor was the leading cause of the conflict. The Southern states thrived on agricultural exports thanks to the expansive lands and the use of slaves in the farms. The slaves were deemed assets in the South (Historical Statistics, 1949). Most of the Northern population felt that slave labor was inhumane and wrong. The southern farmers and the elite, on the other hand, felt threatened because slavery was the backbone of their economy. As illustrated in

Figure 1, slaves formed a large part of the economy. Slave labor brought Southern prosperity. All interventions to end the simmering tensions were futile, and the war began in 1861.

War boils down to money. When the first onslaught happened at Fort Sumter, the South and North quickly found ways to fund the war. The North had a diversified economy, and the government gradually increased taxes. In addition, they floated in war bonds which complimented the expanded tax base (Doyle, 2001). Sadly, the Confederate States, on the other hand, had announced an embargo of their products which meant that they did not have enough income to tax (Doyle, 2001). Even though the South accounted for close to a third of United States assets, they lacked liquid assets. The Confederacy then began to print money in a bid to get supplies for the war. The eleven Confederate States introduced the Confederate Dollar in 1861 and started using it as legal tender. The currency was not backed by any assets such as gold, meaning that the currency was simply a credit promissory note. The Confederacy also lacked enough printing equipment and knowledge, making uncomplex currency, with counterfeiters taking advantage of the situation (Doyle, 2001). While the North also printed money, their diversified economy was able to absorb the shock of inflation.

Figure 1

This image shows the flag of the Confederate flying above Fort Sumter in April 1861 when the war began.

Source: Library of Congress, *(reproduction no.LC-DIG-ppmsca-32284)*

At the start of the Civil War, one confederate dollar had a value of one gold dollar. Four months into the war, inflation had risen by 5% (Lerner, 1955). The Confederate Government's money to support the war was mainly from printed cash and borrowed funds from outside the Confederate. Bond sales and taxes were relatively small. When the Union armies conquered Southern territories, the Confederate notes were banned. As a result, the defeated Confederates sent large amounts of money to other confederates. The increased stock of funds prompted the Confederate Government to raise taxes and introduce a holding tax for those in possession of the currency (Lerner, 1955). The population promptly spent the money to avoid the tax, which increased the prices of commodities. The North further isolated the defeated confederates, stifling output and foreign trade. The increased cash flow, reduced production, and diminished foreign trade resulted in unprecedented inflation. As illustrated in Figure 2, the price of shoes spiked over the course of the civil war. A year after the war started, prices had more than doubled. Between 1863 and 1865, prices continued to rise extraordinarily. When the war ended, the Confederate currency was worthless. The populace had begun engaging in barter trade or even using Union currency to purchase commodities.

Figure 2

The prices of shoes during the War.

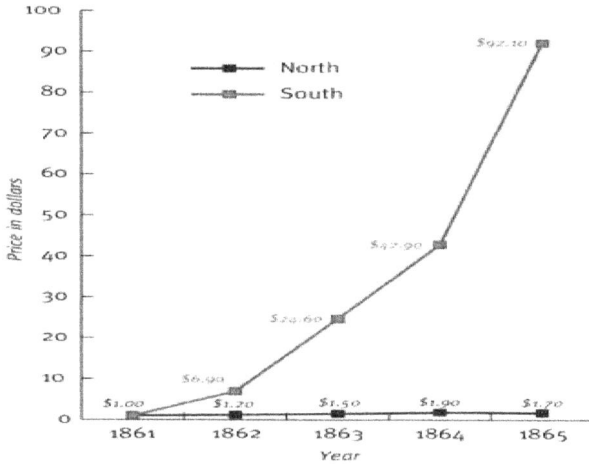

Source: Doyle (2001).

While the Confederate government mismanaged the inflation crisis, partly because of the economy's structure, the Union economy seemed to have reinvented itself. The Union economy expanded and improved during the war. The Union government introduced a raft of measures to win the war and stabilize the economy. The confederate government, before the war, had adopted a constitution that emphasized the autonomy of the different member states (Lerner, 1955). The institution of slavery was also unequivocally protected.

Conversely, the Union government adopted Acts such as the National Banking Act, Homestead Act, and the Railroad Act (Lerner, 1955). The Acts revolutionized tax, land, education, and financial systems. The National Banking Act embraced a national currency that banks backed. This way, the Union could effectively fund the war through government bonds, new taxes, and printing money. The Confederate financed the war by printing money, contributions such as horses and food, bonds, and taxes.

Figure 3

How the North and the South financed the War.

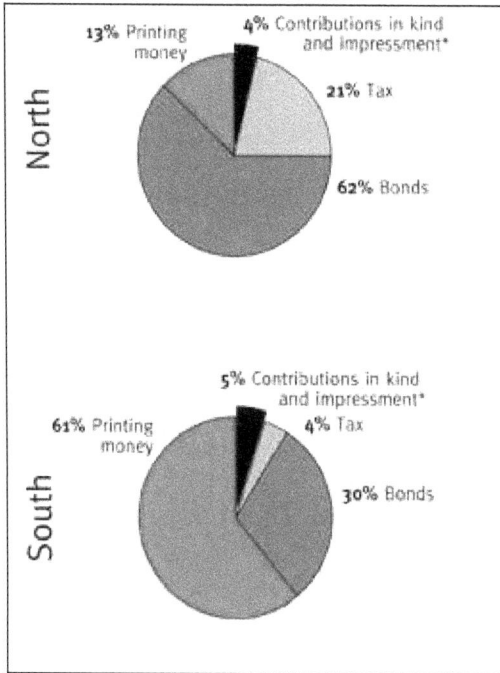

North

13% Printing money
4% Contributions in kind and impressment*
21% Tax
62% Bonds

South

61% Printing money
5% Contributions in kind and impressment*
4% Tax
30% Bonds

Source: Doyle (2001).

Inflation happens all over the world. How a government handles it is what makes the difference. The US Civil War (1861-1865) gives a unique case study of inflation and hyperinflation. The Confederate

53

government did not only lose the war but also ended up with a crippled economy. Both opponents were formidable, and it was expected that they would have similar approaches to fund the war as the decision-makers had worked together in the past. However, this was not the case. The Union government pursued a long-term strategy, introducing taxes on previously zero-rated commodities, licenses, and income. Government credibility paved the way for a dynamic bond market. The union further slashed non-interest-bearing notes that became instrumental in stifling inflation.

On the other hand, the Confederate government adopted a more short-term approach. The regime relied heavily on non-interest-bearing notes. Taxes introduced by the Southerners were unpopular among the masses, making it challenging to collect. In a bid to mask the unpopular taxes, the Confederacy put more emphasis on printing money and bonds. The majority of the banks in the South encouraged speculation by being lenient. The banks issued reckless loans to customers. In the end, the currency became redundant and was declared worthless. As a result, Inflation was a significant problem throughout the war, eventually leading to a total collapse of the southern economy.

A Short message from the Author:

Hey, are you enjoying the book? I'd love to hear your thoughts!

Many readers do not know how hard reviews are to come by, and how much they help an author.

I would be incredibly thankful if you could take just 60 seconds to write a brief review on Amazon, even if it's just a few sentences!

>> Click here to leave a quick review

Thank you for taking the time to share your thoughts!

Your review will genuinely make a difference for me and help gain exposure for my work.

WEIMAR REPUBLIC HYPERINFLATION

Another significant example of hyperinflation was during the early 1920s in the Weimar Republic (Germany). In the era following the end of World War I, Germany witnessed its worst hyperinflation in history. For several months, citizens fought price inflation so bad that entire people's life savings were reduced to the cost of an apple. The state's strategy of financing the war by borrowing heavily and printing vast amounts of unsupported currency started the inflationary spiral. Germany suffered the loss of resources and reparations as mandated by the Treaty of Versailles and political conflict. During World War I, the amount of the German currency had increased fourfold. By 1923, it had risen by billions. From 1914 to 1923, the German currency fell from around four against the USD to one trillion, as shown in Figure 1 (Amadeo, 2020). Initially, the government's fiscal policy lowered the cost of exports and increased economic growth. After the war, the Allied Forces mandated Germany to pay 132 billion marks in war compensations. Production declined in Germany, causing a shortage of commodities. Because of increased money circulation, the prices of essential commodities doubled every four days. In 1923, the inflation rate was 20.9% a day (Amadeo, 2020). It eroded the cash savings of the middle class and caused foreign exchange rates to rise steeply, disrupting commercial activity. By November, the German economy had collapsed completely, and only foreign loans and the issuing of a completely new currency called the Rentenmark reinstated confidence and ended the crisis (The Weimar Republic, 2021).

Figure 1. *Value of German currency against the US Dollar*

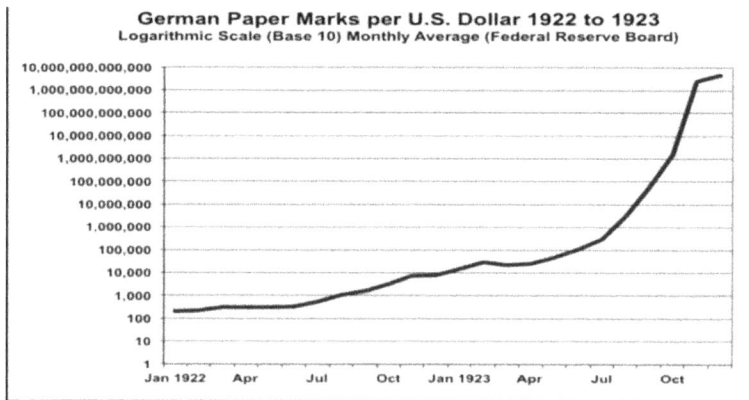

German Paper Marks per U.S. Dollar 1922 to 1923
Logarithmic Scale (Base 10) Monthly Average (Federal Reserve Board)

(Source: Economics Help, 2019)

The Leadup

There are various reasons why Germany entered hyperinflation in the early 1920s. One of the primary reasons is the elimination of goods in the international economy. Before World War I, the global monetary structure was on the gold standard, with the value of major currencies fixed to gold. The Weimar Republic got rid of the gold standard at the onset of the war in 1914 to provide additional financial

(Salemi, n.d). The result was the currency losing its real money balance index, as shown in Figure 2. The real money balance below is an indication of the quantity of goods and services in the economy.

Figure 2. *Fall of the real money balance and an increase in inflation.*

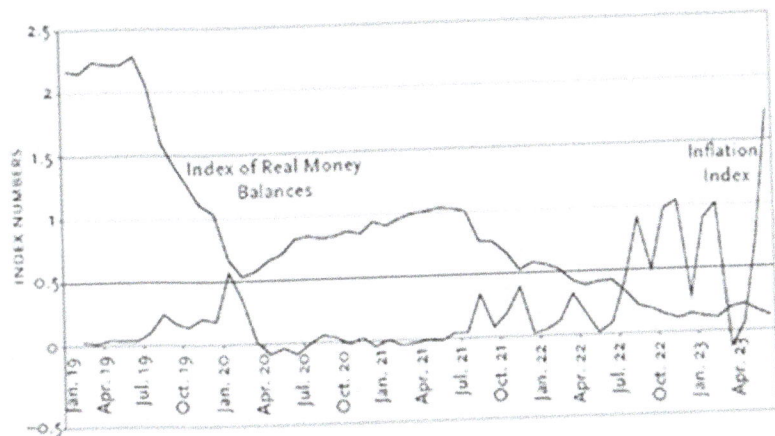

Source: (Econlib)

In January 1923, the Mark was further weakened by the French occupation of the Ruhr in reaction to non-payment of reparations. French and Belgian soldiers occupied Ruhr and the industrial region of Germany in the Ruhr valley. This was to ensure that the nation paid reparations with commodities like coal since the Mark was worthless (Salemi, n.d). The decrease in state revenue caused further strain on state finances, encouraging the German government to print more

flexibility during the crisis. Before the war, a third of the banknotes issued were backed by gold as per the central bank's regulations, limiting the money supply. However, when Germany eliminated the gold standard, the amount of paper money increased considerably, from 2 billion marks in 1913 to 45 billion in 1919, ushering in inflation. During World War I, the cost of living increased threefold.

Another factor that led up to the inflation was the Treaty of Versailles. Under the agreement, the Weimar Republic lost a lot of population and territory. The country was forced to part with considerable reparations, estimated at 6.6 billion pounds. Germany was mandated to pay annual installments of 100 million pounds (Pettinger, 2021). However, collecting this money proved to be a continuous struggle for the state and undermined the currency.

Political instability also played a pivotal role in facilitating hyperinflation. After World War I, Germany experienced close to 400 political murders between 1919 and 1922 (Amadeo, 2020). This escalated political risk and facilitated surging inflation.

As World War I came to an end, Germany entered a period of economic crisis. In November 1918, masses of Germans took control of Germany's cities, angry at the living conditions and demanding an end to the war (Haffert, Redeker & Rommel, 2019). They toppled Kaiser Wilhelm II's monarchy. When millions of German soldiers returned from the Western Front, they joined an ever-increasing class of unemployed citizens in the country. Some turned into troops for the revolutionary far left, some supporting the new liberal government, and some joining the far right. In February 1919, more than one million Germans were unemployed, and the number continued to escalate.

Consequently, the nation experienced a rise in street violence as the revolutionary and the counter-revolutionary factions clashed. In addition to the internal disputes, the country was severely affected by the 1919 Treaty of Versailles that mandated it to pay an unprecedented amount of war debt (Haffert, Redeker & Rommel, 2019). Germany was to pay reparations equivalent to half a trillion USD to the allies. As a result, products, livestock, and raw resources like iron and coal started to be confiscated from Germany as compensation. As a response to the loss of physical and financial resources, the Weimar government constantly printed banknotes with nothing to back them. This approach started to devalue the German currency. After making its first repayments, the value of the German currency declined drastically, ushering in hyperinflation. In February 1922, 160 German marks equaled one USD, and by November 1923, the value had depreciated to 4,200,000,000,000 German marks to one USD (Amadeo, 2020).

First Signs of Hyperinflation

The journey from inflation to hyperinflation accelerated in 1921. In July 1921, Germany experienced a 505% increase in official food prices. Between 1914 and 1922, prices of eggs increased 180 times, while a liter of milk increased from 7 marks in April 1922 to 26 marks in September. In July 1922, prices increased by 50% per month (*Lessons from the past*, 2021). In 1923, inflationary pressures intensified as prices were rising every few hours.

Barter became a prevalent method of trade grounded on products, such as brass and fuel. For instance, a movie ticket could be traded for a lump of coal (*Lessons from the past*, 2021). Similarly, there were narratives of individuals ordering meals in hotels and being charged more when the bill came. During this period, the German currency collapsed as its supply rose drastically. Between November 1918 and November 1923, the currency value fell from 7.4 Marks per USD to 2.5 trillion Marks per USD (*Lessons from the past*, 2021).

Hyperinflation Years

At the start of August 1921, Germany started purchasing fo currency with its mark at any price. However, the move only incre the rate of breakdown in the value of the Mark. In early 1921, th German currency stabilized at around 320 marks per USD (*Less from the past*, 2021). Global reparations conferences compleme this. However, these conferences failed to establish a workabl causing inflation to become hyperinflation as the German cur to 8,000 marks per USD in December 1922, as depicted in F

currency to continue paying off its reparations, sparking off hyperinflation.

We can follow the hyperinflation using banknote denominations. Immediately after the occupation of Ruhr in 1923, the 100000- and 1-million-mark notes were printed. By July the same year, a 50-million mark was issued, and by September, a 500-million note had been issued. In October, the entire value of banknotes in circulation amounted to 2,490,833,908,038,000,000 marks (Hanke, 2007). By November, the central bank printed a 100-million-mark note, marking the peak of hyperinflation. Throughout the hyperinflation era, the printers worked day and night.

Consequently, the German currency became worthless. The hyperinflation continued because of a lack of political will to stop it. The fear of extreme poverty caused higher unemployment and increased political conflict. In October 1922, share prices hit rock bottom as the stock market had declined by 97% from its 1913 level (Hanke, 2007).

As the economy collapsed, Germany started to fall apart. Riots and theft broke out around the nation, with unemployment rising to over 24% in October 1923 (Hanke, 2007). Revolts against central authority erupted in Bavaria and Saxony, leading to the launch of separate currencies by cities that threatened the country's long-term existence. The existential danger to the German state eventually stimulated politicians to act. In October 1923, an enabling law was enacted, allowing the government to legislate without Reichstag`s permission, making Germany a temporary dictatorship. On 17th October 1923, a new central bank called the Rentenbank was established (Hanke, 2007). In November, they introduced a new currency at an exchange rate of 1-trillion old paper marks to one new Rentenmark. They halted the printing of old Marks and controlled the supply of the new currency and state expenditures. By September 1924, the country had a stable currency, ushering in the end of the hyperinflation.

Consumer Behavior during Hyperinflation

The hyperinflation significantly lowered the quality of life for Germans since most worked stable jobs in factories. It led to food shortages, rioting, poverty, and political instability. It intensified corruption, tax evasion, currency speculation, and anti-foreign lobbying. The exponential rise in prices made it hard for ordinary people to acquire essential commodities, such as bread and meat. There are many instances of Germans rushing to the bakery during their lunch breaks because their money would depreciate by the end of the day to a point where they could not afford essential commodities (Goodell, 2018). By September 1923, Germans required enormous amounts of paper money for essential goods. It was a common occurrence to see people carrying buckets or wheelbarrows full of banknotes. Banknotes became worthless to the point that some Germans started using them as wall papers and as toilet paper (Goodell, 2018).

Figure 3. *A German Carrying Stacks of Money with a Wheelbarrow*

Source: (Keripardon, 2013)

The hyperinflation led to a significant redistribution of wealth in Germany. Those dependent on fixed salaries or pensions witnessed a collapse in income, and those with local savings lost everything. At the same time, rents fell close to zero, diminishing the income of landlords. Additionally, urban centers starved as farmers refused to accept paper currency in payment and deferred selling their produce, expecting better prices, causing disputes between cities and the nation. Two million individuals emigrated from towns and cities to the countryside during the inflationary era.

Hyperinflation led to an enormous trade in physical assets. At the start of the hyperinflation, many foreigners took advantage of the collapse of the German mark to purchase German goods in foreign currency. The middle class was mandated to dispose of their possessions when incomes collapsed. However, any individual with debt benefitted as debts were inflated to nothing. For instance, a German landowner who took a loan to buy a property in March 1922 could manage to repay it during the autumn with the sale of less than half a carrot (*Lessons from the past*, 2021). Similarly, the government benefitted since its debts were inflated away.

The Deleveraging

The hyperinflation era continued until 1924, when the coalition government introduced a new temporary currency, renegotiated debt payment to the Allies, and secured new American loans to fund state institutions (*Lessons from the past*, 2021). After introducing the new currency, the Rentenmark, to replace the worthless Reichsbank marks in November 1923, prices in the new currency across Germany remained stable. The move to introduce a new currency was seen as a miracle by Germans as previous intervention efforts only led to more inflation. The new currency was issued at a fixed amount and was backed by physical assets like agricultural land and industrial assets. In August 1923, Karl Helfferich suggested introducing a new currency backed by mortgage bonds indexed to market prices of rye grain (*Lessons from the past*, 2021). However, the proposal was rejected because of the fluctuating cost of rye with the German currency. Then, the agricultural ministry suggested a different proposal that substituted gold for rye. Gold could be traded with a new currency, the Rentenmark, backed by bonds connected to the market prices of gold. Gold bonds were made at a rate of 2,790 gold Marks per kilogram of gold. Here, the new currency was not redeemable in gold but only indexed to the gold bonds. The Rentemark proposal was implemented into the monetary reforms of October 1923 that established a new bank called the Rentebank (*Lessons from the past*, 2021).

From November 1923, the old central bank, the Reichsbank, was not permitted to discount any government treasury bills, thus stopping the printing of paper marks. The discounting of commercial trade bills was allowed, and the amount of Rentenmarks increased. However, the printing of the Rentenmark was firmly regulated to adhere to existing commercial and state transactions. The new central bank denied credit to the state and speculators who could not borrow Rentenmarks since Rentenmarks were not legal tender. By the end of November, there were 500 million Rentenmarks in circulation, which grew to 1000 million by the start of 1924 and 1,800 million in July 1924 (*Hyperinflation in Weimar*, n.d).

Meanwhile, the old currency remained in circulation. By July 1924, the old German Mark has increased to 1,211 quintillion and continued to decline in value to one-third of their conversion value in Rentenmarks. In August 1924, a new monetary law allowed the exchange of the old 1 trillion Mark notes for one Rentenmark (*Hyperinflation in Weimar*, n.d).

Ultimately, some of the debts were restored to moderately reimburse those who had been creditors. In 1925, an order restored some mortgages at 25% of the face value of the new currency if they were held for more than four years. At the same time, some government bonds were restored at 2% of face value after reparations were made (*Hyperinflation in Weimar*, n.d). Here, the restoration of several debts, combined with the recommencement of effective taxation in the crippling economy, prompted a wave of company bankruptcies.

One of the most significant stabilization factors during hyperinflation is revaluation, which involves raising the exchange rate of one currency against other currencies. It also entails the restoration of the value of a currency depreciated by inflation. The German government had the option of either enacting a revaluation law to address the hyperinflation rapidly or to address sprawling and political violence on the streets. The state asserted that the interests of creditors and debtors had to be just and balanced. As such, neither the living standard price index nor the share price index were deemed viable inflation measures. The conversion relation to the dollar index and wholesale price index was better used as a gauge. Here, the government adhered to market-orientated reasoning that the dollar and wholesale price indexes would offer the actual price level during the high inflation and hyperinflation era. The revaluation was grounded on the exchange rate between the Mark and the USD.

Despite the end of the inflation, Germany's nightmare had only just begun. Although the hyperinflation did not usher Hitler to power, it provided a breeding ground for extremism. It would be ten years before Hitler came to power, but many scholars assert that hyperinflation nurtured the seed of Nazism.

Inflation in Ancient Rome

Regarded as one of the strongest empires in history, Rome ruled a quarter of the world at its peak. For three centuries, Rome stood as an indestructible force, with its large armies, stellar governance, and trade surpluses playing a central role in its growth. Therefore, its fall had a resounding impact on global economics, given that the empire was a critical trading partner with other nations. Today the alphabet, calendar, architecture, and languages are highly influenced by the Romans. Experts regard Rome's size and consequent administrative costs as one of the primary reasons for its downfall. Others consider rampant corruption, moral decay, and constant attacks from German barbarians as contributing factors to Rome's downfall. However, there is the economic aspect with taxation, trade, and currency exchange taking center stage. This chapter looks into the great inflation in ancient Rome as one of the primary contributing factors to its downfall.

The Leadup

The Roman Empire enjoyed prosperity and expansion for over three centuries. The growth in size, armies, and economic development played a pivotal role in its establishment. Consequently, it was critical in the empire's downfall, given that when the expansion reached optimum levels, trade reduced, and scarcity of resources kicked in (Butcher, 2015). Inflation in the Roman Empire was subject to several elements, including fluctuations in labor supply and availability of precious metals. The empire's reliance on slave labor had critical implications when it slowed down conquests towards the third century.

The rise of the rival Germanic Barbarians, whose primary aim was freeing slaves, led to a reduced labor supply. Warfare and technological advancement were also central aspects affecting the Empire's ability to maintain its currency circulation and consequent economic stability (Bhardwaj, 2020). These elements had critical implications on pricing and later led to hyperinflation in the region.

It is vital to point out that the Roman Empire anchored its economy on a system of multiple currencies. They borrowed this system from the Greeks, with weights and measures playing a central role in currency valuation. The silver coins, also known as the Denarius, and gold coins, known as Aureus, were the primary currencies. Additionally, the empire used copper and bronze columns with less value and limited centralization when minting. According to Butcher (2015), the army was responsible for the minting of coins and consequent circulation. The soldiers were incentivized to increase their salaries with additional money supply. During the first and second centuries, the empire enjoyed relative peace and prosperity, which were critical for economic stability (Horesh, 2020). However, infighting, corruption, and a breakdown in moral values paved the way for the catastrophe that was about to befall the Roman empire.

Figure 1. *Rome's Denarius silver coins*

Source: (Butcher, 2015).

In the years leading to inflation, the Roman Empire experienced several notable events. From 160 AD to 185 AD, the empire suffered one of the worst plagues in history, that significantly reduced its population size. Then came the frequent usurpations and the auction of the imperial seat in 193 AD (Horesh, 2020). These events had critical implications on political stability, which had ripple effects on the empire's agricultural economy and trade. As mentioned earlier, military setbacks, especially those orchestrated by Barbarian invasions, further weakened the kingdom limiting its conquests and ability to gain access to resources. There were also rising administrative costs, riots from citizens, and increased bread-dole costs, which further complicated the situation. These events led to the emperor's decision to debase the currency to increase currency volume despite the loss of gold and silver from mines and conquests (Horesh, 2020). Therefore, the currency debasement was the principal cause of inflation as the leaders looked to continue appeasing the armies, urban population and tackle fiscal deficits.

The First Signs

From 160 to 274 AD, the empire reduced its gold and silver coins significantly. The lack of the required raw materials coupled with the empire's political, social, and economic situation prompted its leaders to reduce the minting costs by reducing the purity of the currency coins. During this period, the silver coin decreased in purity from 95% to 2% (Andreu & Blanco-Pérez, 2019). With the drastic reduction came an increased circulation of worthless coins in the economy. Additionally, the government raised taxes to increase revenue, increasing the available revenue the government could spend. In retrospect, these aspects increased the amount of wealth held by the elite while increasingly oppressing the poor. This transfer of wealth and an increase of coins of poorer quality into the economy had adverse implications on prosperity (Stange, 2021). It meant that people paid more for the same products. These were the early signs of hyperinflation whereby more coins of poor quality caused higher costs for purchasing goods.

Figure 2. *The debasement of the silver coins 64AD to 288AD*

Silver content of a Roman denarius

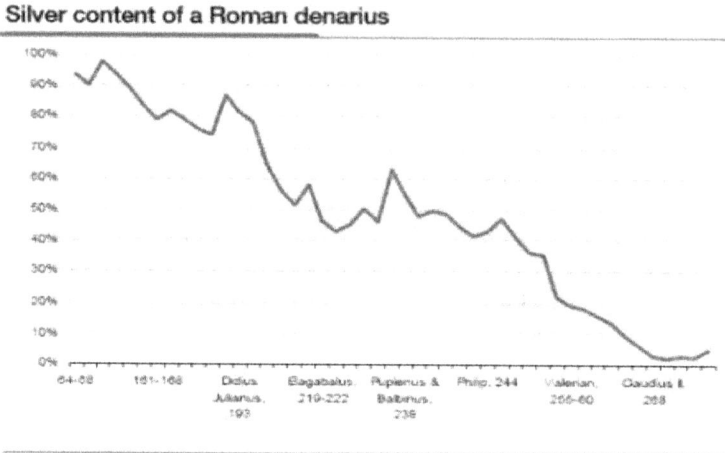

Source: http://www.tulane.edu/~august/handouts/601cprin.htm

Source: (Stange, 2021).

Runaway inflation was also evident with the increase in wages and salaries. People and especially the soldiers, demanded more, given that the quality and value of the coins were decreasing. In 210 AD, Emperor Caracalla raised the soldiers' wages by 50 % (Andreu & Blanco-Pérez, 2019). By 274 AD, only Barbarian mercenaries were paid using gold coins (whose purity was not debased like silver coins).

Another critical problem was ineffective price controls, which further drove the economy into a freefall. Black market activity increased significantly, with barter taking center stage as the silver coins continued becoming worthless. Despite the emperors' attempts to salvage the situation, Rome's toxic hyperinflation cycle continued. For example, in 301 AD, Diocletian introduced a new coin equal to 50 Denarii (Stange, 2021). However, within a decade, the coin's value had plummeted, and it was now equal to 100 Denarii.

The Great Inflation Years

Runaway inflation played a significant role in Rome's downfall. The inflation started around 160 AD, and from then onward, it was an economic and political free fall. It is plausible to claim that these were the inflation years; they were characterized by rampant poverty for the lower classes and increasing wealth for the ruling elite. It is vital to point out that while the silver coin purity decreased drastically, gold coin purity remained strong. Despite using the gold coins to pay Barbarian mercenaries, the ruling elite hoarded gold coins keeping them away from ordinary citizens (Stange, 2021). They, therefore, lived opulent lifestyles while the ordinary citizens continued bearing the burden of hardships.

Additionally, during this period, the ruling elite moved away from exchanging goods through barter trade and adopting the currency system. Earlier, they exchanged goods in the form of land, horses, and slaves. Their adoption of the currency system further increased money circulation in the economy, thereby fostering runaway inflation.

However, it is vital to indicate that loyalty to the emperor slowed the inflation process and made it last centuries. Despite the reduction in the purity of the silver coin, ordinary citizens trusted the government. They, therefore, did not devalue the currency as fast as the quality of the coins declined; this played a crucial role in prolonging the inflationary period and hindering the ability to salvage the situation. During the inflationary period, increased taxation was the order of the day. The government looked to continue with its development programs while supporting its vast army and ever-rising administrative costs. There was also a decline in resources due to an inability to expand the empire further (Parsons, 2010). In addition, there was significant political instability whereby leadership was free for all. The strong usurped the throne, killing leaders and eliminating the element of legitimacy when it came to leadership. Each emperor came with different tactics for tackling inflation, with many achieving little, if any. The deteriorating leadership eventually fueled hyperinflation rates with the devaluation of the currency reaching 1000% by the time Rome crumbled (Parsons, 2010).

Figure 3. *The debasement of Rome's currency system owing to a scarcity of resources*

Figure 1: Metallic content of Roman coins, 160-280 AD

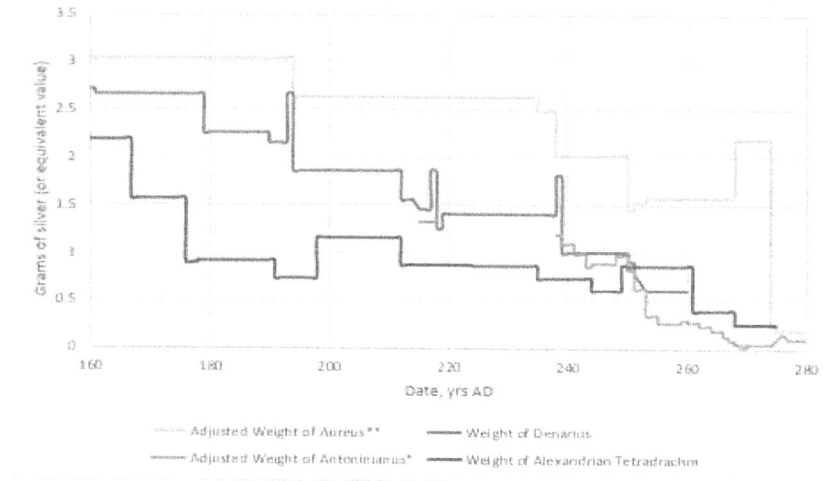

Source: (Parsons, 2010)

The inflationary years had a lasting implication on Rome's trade. Worthless currency, soaring taxes, and a significant increase in the price of goods and services led to the dissolution of the empire's economy (Heather, 2018). With trade decreasing at an alarming rate, the economy became paralyzed, and the empire began collapsing. With no meaningful medium of exchange, barter was the primary form of trade.

By the 3rd century, decades of high inflation had reduced Rome to a lame duck, barely resembling the strong empire it was before. Many dove into the black market since engaging in free trade became a dangerous activity.

Trade networks disintegrated, and the exchange of goods and services remained local. Constant civil wars and uprisings further destabilized the empire. The empire split into three states. It was a free for all, given that political instability crippled the leadership. For example, from 234 to 284 AD, there were about 50 emperors, many of whom were killed in battle, assassinated, or murdered by usurpers (Heather, 2018). Therefore, the inflationary years brought about hardships that had significant implications on the fall of the ancient Roman Empire.

Figure 4. *The decline in the silver value of Denarii fueling*

hyperinflation

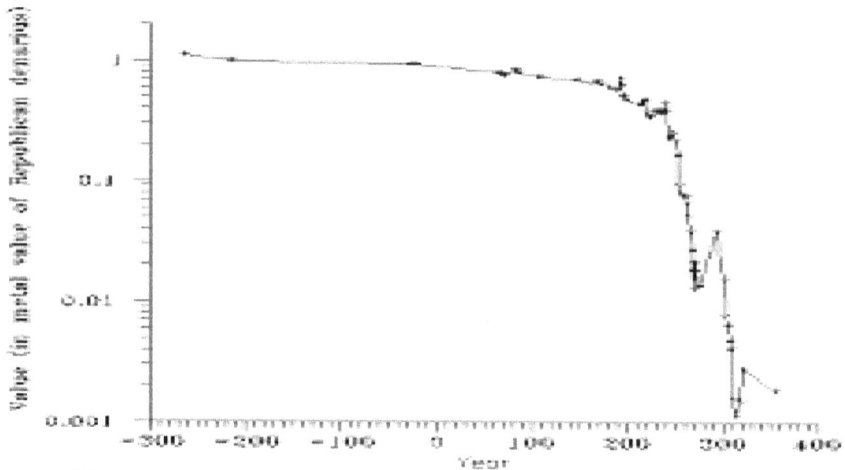

Fig. 4: The natural (silver) value of denarius.
Ag/Cu=61. Scale: New Republic denarius is 1.

Source: (Andreu & Blanco-Pérez, 2019).

How the Common Man Fared During the Inflationary Period

As mentioned earlier, the common man suffered the most during

the inflationary period. They had to deal with the rising prices of goods,

limited resources, and ever-increasing taxation. The quality of life went

on a sharp decline with the increase in the price of goods and services.

To keep from paying more, people hoarded goods and therefore created shortages. Individuals had currency but few goods to purchase. Daily supplies such as wheat, wine, and milk also became scarce, throwing the economy into turmoil. An important aspect to point out is that the ruling elite felt extraordinarily little hardship during inflation. They continued increasing their wealth, especially with the gold coin's slow debasement, which was the primary medium of exchange for the ruling class (Butcher, 2015). As prosperity continued decreasing, the commoner struggled to survive, which led to a lack of trust towards the government and a consequent rise in crime.

It is significant to point out that during the inflationary period, lawlessness increased significantly. Apart from the hoarding of goods and consequent scarcity, there was the issue of government welfare programs. Bread-dole, the government's welfare programs providing bread to its poorest citizens, became a tall order. Therefore, it had to do away with the program since government expenditure kept rising rapidly. This caused significant civil unrest and rioting as the common man started going hungry (Andreu & Blanco-Pérez, 2019). It led to internal strife, which had long lasting effects on the relationship between the government and its citizens.

Additionally, the disintegration of trade networks increased black market activity, which was only affordable to the wealthy. Therefore, the common man went through hardships that can only be termed as survival for the fittest. Soldiers became the gods of this era, given that they are the only ones that possessed currency. The government focused on soldiers and the ruling elite at the expense of ordinary citizens, further deteriorating Rome and its ordinary citizens.

Figure 4. *The nobles enjoyed life at the expense of ordinary citizens during the inflationary years*

Source: (He, 2017)

As indicated earlier, Rome was an agricultural economy, and once inflation hit, food production took a sharp downward turn. Large landowners would no longer export agrarian produce due to the breakdown of trade networks (Heather, 2018). They, therefore, delved into subsistence farming and developed sustainable households. Ordinary citizens started moving away from cities searching for food and security, which led to the adoption of a new system of slavery known as coloni. The common man gave away their civil rights and became half citizens owing their allegiance to large farm owners in exchange for farmlands and security. This formed the foundation for the feudal society and hereditary peasantry, which became common during the Middle Ages. It was also the beginning of self-sufficient societies, which later became a problem for the Roman Empire since they were hostile towards the tax collectors (He, 2017). Therefore, the changes brought about by the inflationary years had lifelong implications on the ordinary citizens' mannerisms and way of doing things.

The Deleveraging

Inflation in the Roman Empire remained a thorny issue until its downfall. Emperors tried salvaging the situation in many ways but to no avail. As highlighted earlier, Rome had numerous illegitimate rulers who had little knowledge of governance during this period. They, therefore, put ineffective laws and policies in place, further accelerating inflation. It is vital to point out that despite the measures put in place, the resource scarcity hindered efforts to control inflation (He, 2017). The main reason was the limited amount of silver and the consequent continuous debasement of the Denarii.

Additionally, many opted to increase government spending on armies to buy their loyalty and secure the throne. They increased taxation to increase revenue while eliminating government welfare programs. Additionally, they increased the soldier's salary to buy loyalty, thus failing to stir up economic growth. Dimitrijevic & Golubovic (2017) argue that by 275 AD, they abandoned the silver coin currency as worthless, introducing copper and bronze coins. These new currency systems did little to save the situation, and thus there was a further increase in inflation and deterioration of the economy. By that time, inflation was at 1000%, with the prices of goods and services increasing sharply.

In 284 AD, Diocletian rose to power and put in policies to counter hyperinflation. He first raised the weight of gold coins from 60 to 72 pounds to increase their value. He also introduced new currencies, introducing a silver coin equal to 50 Denarii and a bronze coin equal to

20 Denarii. However, less than a decade later, the coin's value was half the original value, meaning more than 100% inflation during this period. From 312 AD Constantine also made several reforms to help counter inflation (He, 2017). He first introduced a new gold coin that was more debased than the previous one, helping solidify the gold standards. He also raided treasuries of other empires and took treasures from pagan temples. Constantine also introduced taxes on senator estates and merchant's capital. These elements played a pivotal role in increasing the empire's revenue. However, he faced the problem of counterfeit coins, given that by this time, the gold coin was the primary medium of exchange. Constantine accepted payment of taxes in the form of services or in-kind to limit the number of counterfeit coins circulating among soldiers and civil servants (Dimitrijevic & Golubovic, 2017). This did not last long, and inflation persisted until the fall of the Roman empire.

The Roman Empire faced hurdle after hurdle despite putting measures in place to counter inflation. The leaders had to deal with increasing administrative costs coupled with a reduction in the availability of resources. The debasement of the silver coin had long lasting implications on ordinary citizens, and currency exchange using gold coins was not a feasible idea. The elite continued to flourish at the expense of the ordinary citizens, causing erosion of liberty within the empire. People revolted towards the government, creating internal strife, which did not help counter foreign invasion. Therefore, it is accurate to state that inflation crippled Rome's economy and social values, accelerating its downfall.

FRENCH REVOLUTION HYPERINFLATION

When governments find it unmanageable to continue raising taxes or borrowing funds, they have always looked at printing paper money to finance their expanding expenditures. The resulting inflations have frequently weakened the social fabric, ruined the economy, and ushered in revolutions and tyranny. France's hyperinflation during the French Revolution is an excellent example of this aspect. From an economic perspective, the French Revolution was a disastrous era since it ushered in the first hyperinflation in modern times. France also experienced a considerable decrease in output and severe disruption in its markets. Hyperinflation during the French Revolution left a lasting impact on world history since it led to momentous political and social changes.

The Lead Up

Before the French Revolution of 1789, France was a perfect example of mercantilism. No economic activity could occur without state approval and regulation. While the monarch controlled the economy, the royal court amassed national wealth. King Louis XVI's military guard had 9,500 soldiers, and his civilian household had close to 4,000 individuals (Brezis & Crouzet, 1995). Additionally, the king has 128 musicians, 75 religious leaders, and 198 individuals to take care of his body. The nobility and the clergy were exempt from paying taxes, mandating ordinary citizens to cater to the tax burden. In 1774, the state expenditure was 399 million livres, with tax accounting for only 373 million livres, leaving a deficit of around 27 million livres (Brezis & Crouzet, 1995). Consequently, the loans and monetary expansions made by the king contributed to the hyperinflation during the Revolution.

To address state finances, the king appointed a brilliant economist, Anne-Robert-Jacques Turgot, to act as the finance minister. Turgot tried to use his authority to limit government spending and regulation, but he faced stiff opposition from privileged groups. He was eventually fired by the king in 1776 (Brezis & Crouzet, 1995). (Brezis & Crouzet, 1995).

Figure 1. *The chart on French government finances: 1789-1795.*

Expenditures, Deficit and Debt of the French Government: 1789-1795.

(current prices, millions of Livres)

	[1] Government Expenditures G	[2] Debt Services rB	[3] Taxes T	[4] Government Deficit G-T	[5] Debt Financing ΔB	[6] Money Financing ΔM	[7] Land Financing ΔL	[8] Total Debt B	[9] Gov. Deficit ratio of GNP G-T/Y
Year									
1789	656	230	396	260				4500	0.08
1790	657	281	160	497	-93	590			0.16
1791	823	241	234	589	-637	900	326		0.19
1792	1250	204	412	838	-200	760	278	4000	0.20
1793	3532		341	3191		2850	341		0.70
1794	3180		490	2690		2144	546		0.51
1795	16380		1416	14964		14309	655		0.12

Source: (Velde, 1992).

Subsequently, the chaos of the monarch`s finances led to the session of the Estates-Generals. This was followed by the start of the French Revolutions with the fall of Bastille in July 1789. However, the new revolutionary administration was extravagant in its spending, as shown in Figure 1. Vast amounts of money went to public works to create jobs, and 17 million livres were offered to the citizens in food subsidies King Louis XVI faced the mammoth task of financing the budget deficit that emerged from its debts, which stood at 230 million livres in 1789 (Brezis & Crouzet, 1995). At that time, the public became reluctant to increase its debt holding, making it hard to finance France's budget deficit by issuing further debt. The state also could not raise taxes because the citizens were convinced that they were being overtaxed. When the Third Estate entered the National Assembly after the political and social revolution, it faced the same economic predicament.

The new assembly stipulated that evading taxes was illegal and that there would be no rejection of debt. The primary recommendation to address the budgetary problem was to confiscate and sell church property. The rationale behind the confiscation of the church by the new government was to destroy a rival social authority that could check its moral and political power (Trask, 2020). It also appeased the powerful in Paris and overseas by offering a way to fund the enormous debt of the monarchy. Finally, it established a new group of landowners loyal to the revolutionary state. Since the deficit was growing at an alarming rate and the sale of land could not occur in the short term, the state decided to address the problem by issuing a new financial tool, the assignats. In March 1790, the new government voted to issue a new paper currency called the **assignat**.

The government also realized that the sale of church land was not enough to get the financial results it wanted. The sale of all the properties would reduce their selling price, and France lacked enough capital to embark on large-scale purchases. As a final solution to its fiscal insolvency, the state issued a fiat paper currency (Trask, 2020). The government would finance its deficit by issuing the assignat, and after they sold the Church property, they withdrew the assignats. The assignats would be interest-bearing promissory notes secured by the church land (Trask, 2020). As a result, there was a lot of discussion about what form the assignat would take to solve the budget deficit. Some wanted assignats to become money, and some claimed that it was a political action used to manifest France`s national sovereignty. However, others opposed the introduction of the assignats based on economic principles. They asserted that the new currency would depreciate, and further depreciation would follow, leading to a financial crisis. These objections and warnings were overlooked since the state claimed that France had immense wealth in church property to provide security.

Hyperinflation Years

In December 1789, the government passed a decree to establish assignats as financial security to be exchanged for land, but not as a medium of exchange. The new currency issued in large denominations was interest-bearing but had no legal tender.

By April, 400 million assignat were in circulation. In 1790, they lowered the interest rates on assignats, lowered the denominations, and made it legal tender. The Assembly sanctioned the printing of 400 million livres of paper assignats in denominations of 200, 300, and 1,000 livres, bearing three percent interest and receivable for taxes and the purchase of the national properties (Trask, 2020). In character, they were like English exchequer bills or American bills of credit. Supporters argued that the assignats would provide payments to the state creditors, offer a means for the individuals to purchase lands and properties, draw specie out of hiding, and stimulate trade and industry (Trask, 2020). As such, this opened the way to uncontrollable issues like the creation of unsound money. In the summer of 1791, France doubled its assignats to 800 million, which led to currency depreciation, rising prices, speculation, money shortages, and declining savings.

The government decided to address the problems created by inflation with more inflation. Rather than destroying the assignats received from its state properties, it reissued them in the form of smaller notes. In June 1791, the state issued another 600 million assignats and another 300 million in December. Consequently, the market value of the assignats fell by over 60% in 1792, mandating the state to issue another 600 million assignats (*France: Inflation and Revolution,* 2016). In April 1792, France declared war against Austria. Here, the government deficit increased drastically due to military spending, and repayment of debt was suspended. In 1793, France sought to finance these expenditures by floating two loans, but this initiative yielded little success (Velde & Weir, 1992). As a result, the state printed more assignats to cover its deficit, ushering in high inflation. The government also attempted to terrorize the citizens into accepting the depreciating assignat.

When inflation started getting out of control, the state put price control measures from June 1793 to December 1794. In June 1793, the government passed the Forced Loan, which severely impacted ordinary citizens. The first price controls affected grain but failed to achieve the desired results. Their failure led to the enactment of a new law in September 1793 that reduced the prices of some essential commodities. These price controls made farmers refuse to sell their produce at fixed prices, leading to a severe food shortage (*France: Inflation and Revolution*, 2016). Consequently, the government reacted by forcing its officials to seize what was available and punish farmers who tried to hoard. However, the assignat still fell by 30% against gold (*France: Inflation and Revolution*, 2016).

Figure 2. *France money supply 1789-1797.*

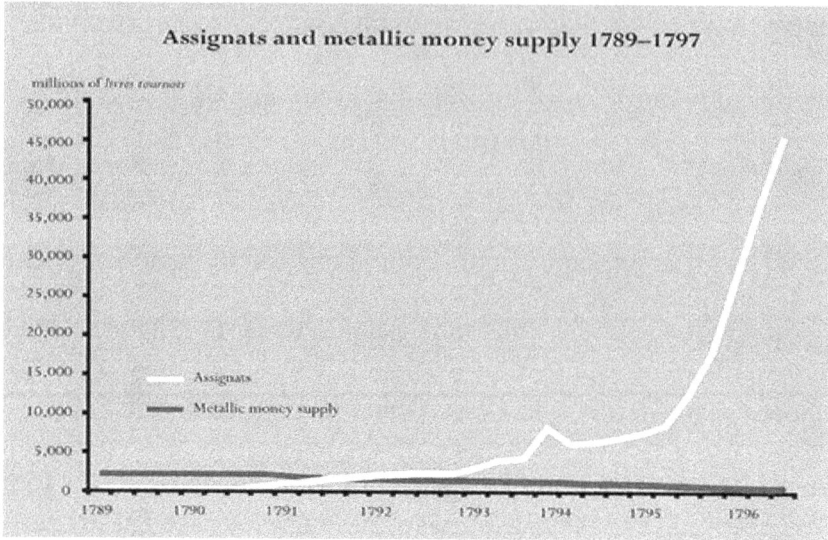

Source: (American Numismatic Society, 2016)

Figure 2 summarizes the pathway to hyperinflation. The state introduced 800 million assignats by mid-1790 despite facing a deficit. By the end of 1791, 1.5 billion assignats circulated the economy, and the purchasing power reduced by 14%. In mid-1793, there were 4.1 billion assignats in circulation, and their value declined by 60% (Trask, 2020). By the end of 1795, 19.7 billion assignats were in circulation, and the purchasing power had depreciated by 99% since the currency

98

was introduced (Trask, 2020). Within five years, the assignats had become worth less than the paper it was printed on.

Impact to Consumers

The impacts of the monetary collapse during this period were enormous. The hyperinflation created many debtors who wanted the inflation because a depreciating assignat meant they repaid in worthless currency. On the other hand, some speculated on land, primarily former Church properties that the state had seized and sold, since their wealth rose with the inflationary increase in land value (Sargent & Velde, 1995). As money became worthless, instantaneous remedies took precedence over long-term thinking. There was a shortage of commodities as sellers hoarded them in anticipation of higher prices in the future. The price increases are illustrated in Figure 3. Soap became so rare that Parisian washerwomen demanded that any vendor who declined to sell their items be executed. In February 1793, crowds in the capital raided around 200 shops, stealing everything from bread to

sugar and clothes (Sargent, & Velde, 1995).

Figure 3. *Food prices during the French Revolution.*

Prices of Food during the French Revolution.

year	Prices in Livres					Price increase %				
	Wheat Château-Goutier [1]	Rye [2]	Wheat Buis [3]	Rye Romans [4]	Wheat Nat. mean [5]	Wheat Château Goutier [1]	Rye Goutier [2]	Wheat Buis [3]	Rye Romans [4]	Wheat Nat. mean [5]
1788	120	81	77	52	1609					
1789	126	102	109	55	2192	5.00	25.93	41.56	5.77	36.23
1790	140	112	118	45	1945	11.11	9.80	8.26	-18.18	-11.27
1791	125	103	105	63	1622	-10.71	-8.04	-11.02	40.00	-16.61
1792	156	111	122	92	2209	24.80	7.77	16.19	46.03	36.19
1793	168	112	150	108		7.69	0.90	22.95	17.39	
1794	233	187				38.69	66.96			
1795										
1796	120	139								
1797		95			1948					

Source: (American Numismatic Society, 2016)

The most affected group by the hyperinflation was the poor.

Financiers, merchants, and commodity speculators who took part in

international trade could safeguard themselves (Ebeling, 2007). They amassed gold and silver, sent it overseas for safety, and invested in other durable commodities, such as art and precious jewelry. Their theoretical knowledge allowed most of them to take advantage of the hyperinflation and profit from the currency fluctuations. Since the working class and the poor have little or no knowledge of protecting themselves, they ended up holding billions of worthless assignats.

Deleveraging

As inflation worsened, there was an appeal by the people to stop the drastic rise in prices. As a result, in May 1793, the National Assembly imposed price controls on grain and stipulated that it could only be sold in public markets under the watch of state officials. They had the power to break into sellers' homes and confiscate hoarded grain and flour (Ebeling, 2007). Similarly, the destruction of goods under state control became a capital offense. In September, they extended the price controls to all essential commodities. It was to escalate prices by more than a third. They also regulated wages. Goods became scarce because farmers declined to sell their produce to cities, leading to a severe food shortage.

During the Jacobin Republic of 1792–1794, numerous regulators moved across the country, imposing price limits and interfering in every aspect of the citizens` lives (Trask, 2020). They enforced death sentences, seized wealth and property, and sent individuals to jail and slave labor. After the revolutionary war, all sectors connected to national defense or foreign trade were put under state control, including production, prices, and distributing of all commodities by private merchants (Trask, 2020). Consequently, an enormous bureaucracy materialized, swallowing up vast portions of the country`s wealth. The state`s rationale was that it had a duty to impose a collective arm for the country's sake. As such, the individual was nothing, and the government was everything.

However, in 1794, an anti-Jacobin government came to power and advocated for a free market. Famers, manufacturers, and merchants would now enjoy complete control of their property, production, and industry. In December 1794, the Government abolished wage and price controls, and the economy was allowed to function as a free market. Although agricultural output increased in 1795, industrial output decreased in some parts. Inflation surged upwards to reach 3500%, which erases a significant portion of the public debt (Trask, 2020).

In December 1795, the state stopped the printing of the assignats, allowing the flow of goods and restoring a degree of prosperity. Additionally, gold and silver transactions were permitted and were legally binding. The state tried a new paper currency called the Mandats Territoriaux to substitute the assignat. By August, the state issued more than 2,500 million Mandats (Ebeling, 2007). People could exchange the currency for land, but it failed to stop inflation. The exchange rate of the assignats to the Mandats was too high, and they had many problems. Within six months, the Mandats Territoriaux had depreciated as much as the assignats had done in six years (Ebeling, 2007). By December 1796, France had returned to specie. It withdrew the Mandat as the legal tender.

However, it took Napoleon to restore hard money in France and to stop the hyperinflation. Napoleon introduced the 20 franc gold piece and stipulated that all government workers and merchants would be paid only in gold or its equivalent, effectively ending the paper blizzard (Trask, 2020).

It was not an accident that the first modern hyperinflation took place in the 1790s. The French Revolution significantly changed how Europeans thought about money. The French government envisioned the assignat as a way for people to conduct business without requiring the transfer of land titles. The move away from older and more physical manifestations of wealth only became prevalent in the 19th century. Although previous generations had been deeply suspicious of paper money, it became appealing because it was easier to ship paper currency over long distances than to transport gold or goods to businesses operating far away (Trask, 2020).

Hence, the development of paper currency is fundamental to comprehending the political, social, and economic outcomes of hyperinflation throughout civilization. The currencies utilized by Europeans before the 1700s had value outside their function as a medium of exchange. Thus, they did not inflate like paper money.

The move towards paper currency significantly altered individuals' relationships with their wealth. Similarly, in our current society, we are witnessing an identical shift in the way we relate to our money. Today, one can use their phone to pay for almost anything without the need for paper money. As we embrace digital currencies like Bitcoin and Cardano, it is fundamental to examine the history of money to gain insight into the connection between innovation in financial technologies and the types of economic crises we face today.

Hyperinflation in Hungary

Hyperinflation in Hungary after World War II in 1946 remains

the most intense ever recorded. Hungary was a part of the Axis powers

that allied with Germany during the war. They lost to the Soviet Union

forces in 1945. In 1944, Hungary was a battleground that suffered

significant losses of over 40000 people, capital, land, and minerals like

gold. The Hungarian economy suffered heavy losses, with all sectors

falling by over 40% in value. Until this point in time, there have been

56 recorded hyperinflation episodes. Numerous individuals had heard

tales of Germany in the mid-1920s, where a loaf of bread cost a barrel

loaded with cash. Be that as it may, not many know about the most

prominent hyperinflation ever, where, at the pinnacle, prices multiplied

every 15.6 hours, and notes were given in divisions of 100 million

pengőes and 1 billion pengőes (He, 2017). This chapter explores

hyperinflation in Hungary, including the lead-up to hyperinflation, the first signs of hyperinflation, the hyperinflation years, how Hungarians faired during the inflationary period, and the deleveraging period.

The Lead Up to Hyperinflation

In post-WWII, Hungarian policymakers had two issues to deal with: inflation and shortage of products. Grossman and Horváth (2000) investigated the choices policymakers needed to make: either urge inflation or attempt to battle it by raising income and cutting currency flow (Kumar, 2015). Eventually, they decided that inflation was the way to help the economy by energizing production before the new currency was presented. Regardless of whether policymakers chose to battle hyperinflation, it might have been unavoidable from the amount of cash in circulation. As Valkovszky and Vincze (2012) clarify, expanding the cash supply was considered as an approach to localize utilization. When there is high inflation, cash loses value and, in this way, individuals are forced to purchase products. Nevertheless, an expansion in the cash supply is only helpful if there are goods to purchase. The government tried this approach to animate production, which had devastating impacts.

The First Signs of Hyperinflation

It is critical to investigate the sectors and areas that were negatively affected by World War II. The worst affected were the coal and rail businesses, as their decrease in production and capital affected monetary recuperation and profitability (Kumar, 2015). The rail line industry was influenced by the conflict; train lines and rail-related enterprises were obliterated. Without coal, there was little power, and production across all ventures were affected.

The lack of capital for constructing railroads hindered the transportation of products and individuals. All local or domestic travel was restricted, and railroads were only used for factory laborers and emergencies. The year 1945 was an incredibly awful one for agribusiness (Kumar, 2020). Hungary encountered a terrible drought, mainly owing to a dry spell: expected wheat production was 3 million tons, while the actual production was just 1 million tons. With lower crop yields, the eating routine of Hungarians changed significantly. All the while, prices of raw materials started to rise due to excessive shortages.

Figure 3. *The cost of living during the onset of hyperinflation*

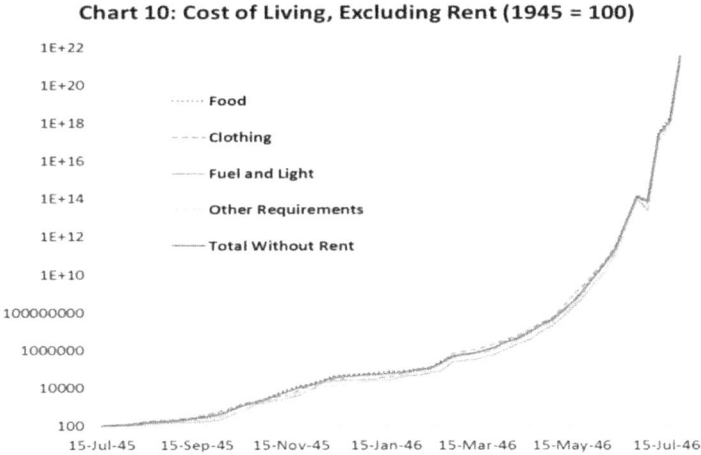

Chart 10: Cost of Living, Excluding Rent (1945 = 100)

Source: (Kumar, 2020)

Regardless of whether for financial or political reasons, most business activity post WWII in Hungary was nationalized and became state undertakings. The mining businesses and few force plants were nationalized before hyperinflation ended (Valkovszky and Vincze, 2012). During hyperinflation, the government needed to work both openly and secretly to empower businessmen, speculation, and production.

To handle rural issues, a significant land change occurred. Land change split up huge settlements and attempted to give lower class individuals private land. The government offered advances in private credit markets at loan fees that were not indexed to inflation. This is because the government realized that the installments would become useless due to inflation (Kumar, 2020). The Hungarian government then urged banks to loan assets to businessmen. The national bank's markdown rate was 3% and representing the inflation that came to more than 10,000 percent, the real interest rates turned out to be negative.

The Hyperinflation Years

This hyperinflation began in Hungary in August 1945 and halted in July 1946, when the Hungarian pengő was supplanted with the Hungarian forint. There were endeavors during the period to balance out the currency, most remarkably with an alternative pengő record, where transformation rates were changed each day to represent rising prices (Valkovszky and Vincze, 2012). Adjustment happened on August 1, 1946, when the Hungarian government provided another currency — the Hungarian forint. The hyperinflation was outrageous to such an extent that the last conversion rate was 400 octillions (4 followed by 29 zeros) pengőes for only one forint. As Figure 1 shows, 1945 through 1948 were the years when hyperinflation was at its highest (Kumar, 2020).

Figure 1. *Retail and Wholesale prices in Hungary before and during*

inflation.

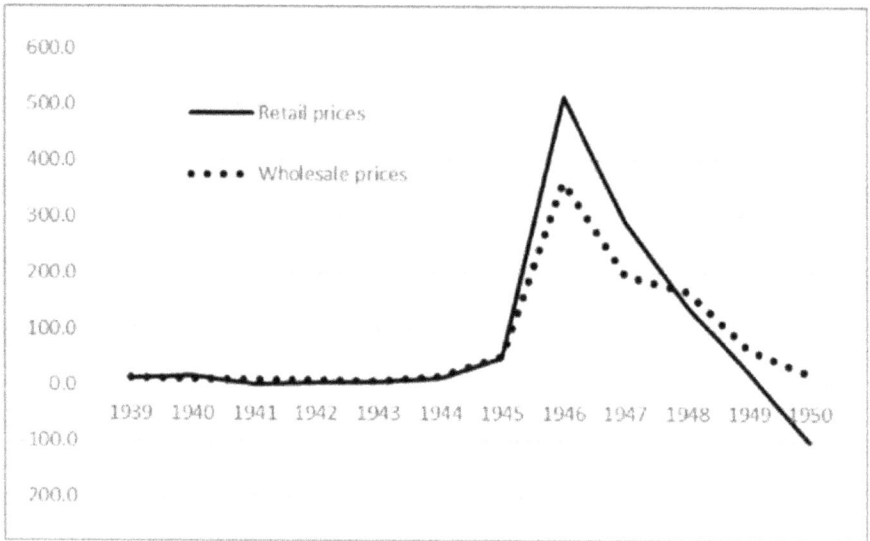

Source: (Kumar, 2020)

Consumer Behavior during the Inflationary Period

Most financial and monetary approaches adopted by the

government had a negative influence on consumer behavior. Although

stakeholders possessed an essential understanding of hyperinflation, the

Government had no experience on the effects of hyperinflation (He,

2017). Both the 1923 and 1946 hyperinflations proved that financial and monetary changes had significant and detrimental effects on consumer behavior.

The prices of consumer goods started rising as the country's production capacity fell. The government took measures to control the sharp rise in prices. Since there was no tax base to rely on, it opted to stimulate its economy by printing more money. Banks were given loans at low rates who then loaned it to citizens and businesses at even lower rates. The government also hired workers directly and gave large amounts of money to people to get its economy running again. The currency in circulation in July 1945 stood at 25 billion Pengö but rose to over 1.6 trillion by the February 1946. By May that year, 65 quadrillion was in circulation and 47 septillions by July 1946 (He, 2017).

Consumers were heavily impacted by the financial measures adopted by government to manage the looming hyperinflation. A commodity that cost 380 Pengö in September 1945 was sold at over

72000 Pengö in January 1946, over 450000 Pengö by February 1946,

over 1.8 million Pengö by March, and over 11 trillion billion Pengö by

July that year (He, 2017). By August 1946, the hyperinflation was

devastating and challenging to consumers. At the peak of

hyperinflation, prices skyrocketed over 150000% daily, making it the

worst in world history (He, 2017). Consumers refrained from paying

taxes altogether since a day's delay in tax collection wiped out the

currency value collected by the government. Prior to the war, 5 Pengö

were equivalent to 1 US dollar. However, by June 1944, 1 US dollar

was equal to 33 Pengö and over 1300 by August 1945 (He, 2017). The

Pengö later collapsed, and 1 US dollar was equal to 10000 Pengo by

November that year, over 1.75 million Pengo by March 1946, 59 billion

Pengo by April 1946, and over 460 septillions by July that year (He,

2017). 1 septillion is 1 followed by 24 zeroes!!!

Clearly, the Hungarian government undertook failed measures

to counter hyperinflation. In December 1945, it imposed a capital levy

of 75% to force consumers to return 400 Pengö and receive 100 Pengo

114

as the legal tender (He, 2017). Nevertheless, it did not stop printing money. The government was forced to introduce the Adopengö as an inflation indexed currency. However, the Adopengö succumbed to the pressures of hyperinflation and was valued at 2 million trillion to a single Pengö (He, 2017).

The situation in Hungary was so critical that the government had to embrace various unique currencies. Printing new currencies was one of the solutions adopted by the government to stabilize the economy and mitigate the effects of the hyperinflation. It started by reducing wages by over 80%, which pushed many people into poverty (He, 2017). Many creditors were wiped out because production and manufacturing failed to recover. This helped the government to achieve its goal of stimulating and reviving production and raising the country's industrial capacity. Most stagnant industries like railroads and factories started working again and replenished the lost capital stock. The main losers were consumers and workers who lost over three-quarters of their wages and lacked credit services since all creditors had been wiped out

(Stojković, 2019).

The Deleveraging

The solution adopted by the government was to change the

currency name. The Pengö was replaced with the Milpengö, which was

equivalent to 1 million Pengö. The Milpengö was replaced by the

Bilpengö which was equivalent to 1000000000000 Pengö (He, 2017).

The situation became so dire that consumers identified notes by their

color and not value. Cashiers would say to consumers that a product

cost one blue and two greens instead of stating the currency value,

which they found confusing. By August 1946, the Forint had replaced

the devalued Pengö and was valued at 400000 Quadrillion Pengö

(Stojković, 2019). 1 Quadrillion is 1 followed by 12 zeroes. However,

later measures relatively stabilized prices and by 1960, all Pengös had

been discarded because they were worthless.

Politically, the fate of Hungary was sealed by the communist regime in 1949, which seized power after the war and changed the Republic of Hungary into the People's Republic of Hungary. The new republic modeled and adopted financial, monetary, and constitutional models similar to those of the Soviet Union.

A Historical Perspective

From 1938-1948, annualized change in GDP per capita was better in Hungary than in Germany, Greece, or Romania. I picked 1948 as the endpoint since it was a couple of years after WWII, giving the affected nations time to recuperate. Nonetheless, both Yugoslavia and Italy performed better than compared Hungary in this period. The annualized change in GDP per capita for Hungary between 1938 and 1946 was higher than in Germany and Greece, however, lower than in Italy (Kumar, 2015). From information on production across sectors, it is obvious that Hungary's economy, regardless of hyperinflation, had the ability to recuperate from WWII.

Figure 4. *100 quintillion (1020) pengő, the largest denomination bill ever issued, Hungary,*

Source - Wikipedia

By 1948, GDP per capita was 83% of pre-war levels. Sectors like coal and railway had recuperated to around comparative levels. Examinations of GDP per capita to close nations show that Hungary had a better recovery than most of her neighbors. This, notwithstanding, doesn't permit us to decide the degree to which hyperinflation influenced their economy.(Kumar, 2015).

The Great Chinese Inflation

Introduction

Inflations have destabilized the cultural and commercial fabric of society, ushering in social disorder and revolt. An excellent example of such inflation is the Great Chinese Inflation between the 1930s and 1940s. The destruction of the Chinese monetary system in this era facilitated Mao Zedong's communist movement to succeed in China. Between 1935 and 1949, China witnessed a great hyperinflation in which prices increased by more than 1000% (Hewitt, 2007). The primary cause of the hyperinflation was the policies of the Nationalist government, as it repeatedly introduced enormous sums of fiat currency into the Chinese economy. After World War II, the monetary expansion undertaken by the state was so severe that the Nationalist printing presses could not keep up. As a result, the government printed Chinese currency in England and flew them over the Himalayas.

Path to Hyperinflation

Before 1935, the Chinese had a restricted free banking system. Privately-owned banks were located across the country, though the leading Chinese banks were in Shanghai. Some provincial governments regulated their banks but had to ensure quality to compete with private banks. These private banks were incredibly competitive and operated largely without government regulation. Although coins were made of copper, silver was used as the primary medium of exchange, and the Chinese economy operated on an informal silver standard. Most banks issued distinct notes which were exchangeable with silver. These notes circulated freely with other banks' notes.

When the Nationalist government assumed power in 1927, it began an extensive process to get rid of free banking in the country, and by 1935, it had accomplished this objective. Instead of complete confiscation, the government followed an incremental strategy to control the currency (Habegger, 1988). The initial measures obtained the political and financial support of the biggest banks in the country. The state was to place Chinese banks under the direct authority of the

Nationalists, eliminating any restrictions due to currency regulation. Ultimately, all banks would rely on the state.

In 1927, the process started when banks got involved in the political conflict between the Nationalists and the Communists (Hewitt, 2007). As a result, violent walkouts headed by Communist leaders crippled the economy in Shanghai. And when bankers ask the state for help, the Nationalists government took this chance to strengthen its financial position. It made an agreement with bankers to subdue the strikes in exchange for loans to the state. Banks thought that the Nationalist government would be more supportive of their operations than a Communist regime.

Consequently, they became a fast source of money for the Nationalist regime and firm supporters even though the banks were losing their autonomy. Gradually, banks became worried about the state's capacity to repays its growing debt. Bankers declined to lend the government more money, and the state reacted by employing the same approach against bankers it had applied against the strikes. Bankers who refused to supply loans were arrested, and their properties confiscated.

In 1928, the Nationalist government established the Central Bank of China as an extension of the Treasury. The Central Bank started providing private banks with vast quantities of bonds secured by the state revenue from custom taxes with high interest rates. However, these bonds only made the financial scenario worse. In 1931, Japanese troops captured Manchuria and formed the puppet government Manchukuo. The capture of Manchuria was a devastating blow to the Nationalists because the area had a massive prospect for industrial development. As a result, government bonds went for around 50% of their face value. In 1932, Chinese banks in Shanghai held between 50% to 80% of outstanding government bonds (Ebeling, 2010). To improve public perception, the state appointed numerous directors of private banks to work alongside Central Bank directors. However, they had little or no authority.

Between 1929 and 1932, China battered a global financial and economic hurricane and witnessed an export explosion. Domestic prices increased while the rest of the planet underwent a profound price deflation. In September 1931, Great Britain got rid of the gold standard. Many nations embarked on currency depreciation, which undesirably impacted the worth of the Chinese silver dollar in the financial markets. However, the disastrous shock came in 1933 and 1934 when the United States` president remonetized silver under the New Deal. Here, the US embarked on a silver-purchasing extravaganza at higher prices in an effort to drive a price high in the US (Hewitt, 2007). As a result, silver flowed out from Shanghai, and exports of silver from China to the US increased drastically. This led to a disastrous price deflation that affected China's agriculture and industry. The appreciation of the Chinese currency during the deflationary era increased the government's debt. Consequently, the Nationalist government implemented foreign exchange regulations on silver exports in late 1934.

Figure 1. *Money Supply in China between 1937-1948*

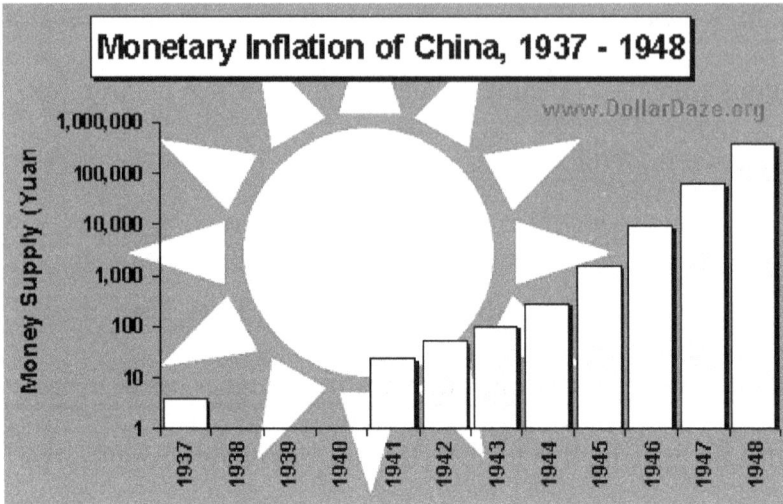

Source (Hewitt, 2007)

First Signs of Inflation

The state gave the Central Bank special rights like an exception from silver export regulations. As a result, the Central Bank became the nation's most lucrative financial establishment in 1937. As the government's finances worsened, it issued the Savings Bank Law, which mandated every private bank purchase government bonds equal to one-fourth of its total deposits (Habegger, 1988). The state started propaganda against the bankers to avert a prevalent bond market collapse. The propaganda blamed the country's economic issues on private bankers. In March 1935, the state clutched control of the two biggest banks in China, the Bank of China and the Bank of Communications. Soon, it utilized the funds from these banks to takeover smaller private banks (Ebeling, 2014). In July 1935, the Nationalist regime had eliminated private banking in the country as it became the majority shareholder in every bank. Despite the enormity of China's biggest banks, the state could not sustain itself. Businesses continued to shut down as more silver was smuggled out of the country.

The end of private banking meant that the resources of the Chinese banks were available to the government as it held a majority share in every bank. As a result, the state immediately used these resources to finance its activities. Banks were mandated to buy state securities and to advance loans. Nonetheless, the banking coup had no impact on the deflation as companies shut down, and more silver was trafficked out of the country. Hence, the state imposed a death or life imprisonment on anyone smuggling silver out of the nation. However, deflation persisted.

With the elimination of private banking, the Nationalist government proposed introducing a controlled currency secured by nothing but state promise assurances. The move to a paper currency was supposed to benefit the state in two ways. First, the state would have control of all silver, which would enable the deflation to stop. Second, the state would have a monopoly over the money supply to make it possible to monetize its debt.

In November 1935, the Central Bank of China issued the Currency Decree, took China off the silver standard, and introduced a fiat currency. The Nationalist government has an absolute monopoly over the money supply, meaning that it could monetize its debt. Only the notes issued by the most prominent government banks were regarded as legal tender. The Central Bank regulated the new fiat currency, called the fai-pai. All institutions and people in possession of silver were mandated to exchange it for the new currency within six months.

To maintain confidence in the new currency, the Currency

Decree contained provisions to create a Currency Stabilization Fund,

which would purchase and sell foreign exchange to keep the rate fixed

relative to specific foreign currencies. The Degree also comprised

provisions that changed the operations of the Central Bank. Rather than

being an extension of the Treasury, the Central Bank became a banker's

bank, different from the Treasury. However, the Decree was a state's

effort to suppress fears of inflation. Chinese media produced articles

aimed at assuring the people that the government was looking at their

best interests. Additionally, the international community endorsed the

shift towards a fiat currency as a step towards a modern banking

system. Nonetheless, the stat never removed the Central Bank from the

Treasury's control.

Hyperinflation Years

The currency reform of 1935 destroyed the private banking

system, which had backed the Chinese economy effectively for decades.

Moreover, with an incompetent and corrupt regime in control of the

Chinese economy, inflation happened immediately. The monetary authority over the currency was a disastrous blow to China's economy. Massive monetary inflation occurred from July 1937 to 1945 to fund the war with Japan (Ebeling, 2010). As a result, about 70% of China's yearly expenditures were covered by newly printed currency. As a result of the severe financial expansions during World War II, Nationalist printing presses could not keep up, and the country had to outsource from Great Britain. Ultimately, inflation worsened and facilitated the collapse of the Nationalist administration.

The war between China and Japan persisted for eight years, from July 1937 to September 1945. Japanese troops occupied about one-third of China, including all the nation's main port cities and industrial hubs. During the war, over ten million Chinese died fighting. In 1945, a longstanding civil war broke out between Chiang Kai-shek's Nationalist government and the large communist forces led by Mao Zedong. The conflict continued for four years until the communists emerged victorious and the Nationalist troops retreated to Taiwan in 1949.

During the war with Japan, the Nationalist government decided to print more money to fund its expenditures, covering around 70% of its annual spending via money creation. Between 1946 and 1949, monetary expansion accounted for close to 60% of the state's spending. At the start of the war in 1937, the total amount of money in circulation was 36 billion Yuan. By 1941, the money supply had expanded to 22.8 billion Yuan. This trend continued throughout the war era to 1,506 billion Yuan in 1945.

The civil war worsened inflation. In December 1946, the money supply increased to 9,181 billion Yuan, and by late 1947, it had grown to 60,965 billion Yuan. In July 1948, the money in circulation had risen to 399,091 billion Yuan. Consequently, the government introduced a new currency to replace the old depreciated one at a conversion rate of three million old Yuan for one new currency. The new Yuan was secured by gold. In August 1948, the government stipulated that it would redeem paper Yuan for gold to restore public confidence in the fiat currency (Ebeling, 2014). As a result, thousands of individuals lined up in front of the Bank of China carrying huge bags filled with paper currency to exchange their paper currency for gold. However, the state

seized selling gold the following day. It stipulated that gold, silver, and

foreign exchange ownership were prohibited, and individuals had to

accept the new fiat currency for the old. The new converted money

supply was 296.82 billion Yuan in August 1948, and by April 1949, the

supply of the new currency had increased to 5,161,249 billion Yuan.

Consumer Impact

Between 1937 and 1949, prices increased drastically but at

varying degrees across various parts of the country because of war-

associated scarcities, destructions, and the disastrous effects of the

monetary expansion. By December 1941, the Shanghai wholesale price

index was 15.98. In late 1945, this index had reached 177,088 and by

April 1949 it stood at 151,733,000,000,000 (Ebeling, 2010). The value

of the Chinese currency on the foreign exchange market depreciated

considerably. Before the start of the China-Japan war in 1937, 3.41

Yuan traded for one USD. In 1945, the Yuan traded at 1,222 to the dollar, increasing to 23,280,000 Yuan in May 1949 (*Inflation and CPI Consumer Price Index 1940-1949*, n.d.)

During and after the war, the Nationalist regime enacted unworkable price and wage controls to curb inflation. However, this created more distortions and disproportions in the entire Chinese economy, causing shortages, black markets, and increased corruption. The state's policies created social and commercial unrest that helped the communists since Mao's government promised to eliminate corruption and the violations of the Nationalist regime (Ebeling, 2014). The hyperinflation destroyed the wealth and savings of the ordinary Chinese people and ushered chaos across the economy because of the loss of a reliable and stable medium of exchange. Moreover, inflation and its impacts made a significant portion of the rural population enter severe poverty. As a result, any support the Nationalist regime had in rural areas diminished significantly.

A notable aspect of Chinese hyperinflation is the complete lack of adequate price controls, which contributed to the use of currency as a means of payment. This was different from other hyperinflations throughout history (Ebeling, 2014). For instance, during the German hyperinflation after World War II, extensive price controls made barter an attractive way to trade regardless of its many demerits. The Chinese government did not place effective price controls except for rents and a few commodities rationed and distributed by state agencies in big cities. Since prices could increase freely, financial transactions were not penalized. Hence, consumers used the Chinese currency as the primary medium of exchange throughout the hyperinflation.

The Deleveraging

Saying that the Great Chinese Inflation was the sole cause for the defeat of the Nationalist regime and the triumph of the Communist party would be an exaggeration (Habegger, 1988). The Nationalist government was an authoritarian system, infamous for its corruption and misuse of authority, and relentless in its usage of military power. However, it is evident that whatever support the Nationalist government had gained against the communist, particularly among China's middle class, was extensively damaged by the inflation.

The Chinese experience from 1935 to 1949 revealed that individuals might retain currency as a medium of exchange under hyperinflation but discard it as a store of value and unit of account (Ebeling, 2010). Numerous scholars have thought that under such conditions, the usage of currency would have seized entirely. However, the Chinese hyperinflation had the opposite impact. Rather than facilitating the collapse, it led to adjustments that lessened the effects of inflation. Depreciation considerably increased the cost of using currency. Still, the Chinese were willing to pay a high price to avert the drawbacks of barter and price regulations that might have made barter more lucrative than monetary exchange.

Hyperinflation in Yugoslavia

Introduction

The circumstances leading to hyperinflation are often unique to the region. However, most reported cases in history had been influenced by policies that increased money circulation in the economy. When a country experiences an uncontrollable spike in commodity prices followed by devaluing of the national currency against others, it faces hyperinflation. The consumer's purchasing power reduces due to the inability of the buyers to afford the price attached to daily consumables like food.

Excessive money supply creates a scenario where the consumer requires large sums of money to purchase small quantities of commodities in the marketplace. There is an imbalance in the relationship between cash and goods. Such causative factors were witnessed in Yugoslavia during the early 1990s, as Figure 1 shows.

Figure 1. *Yugoslavia Hyperinflation.*

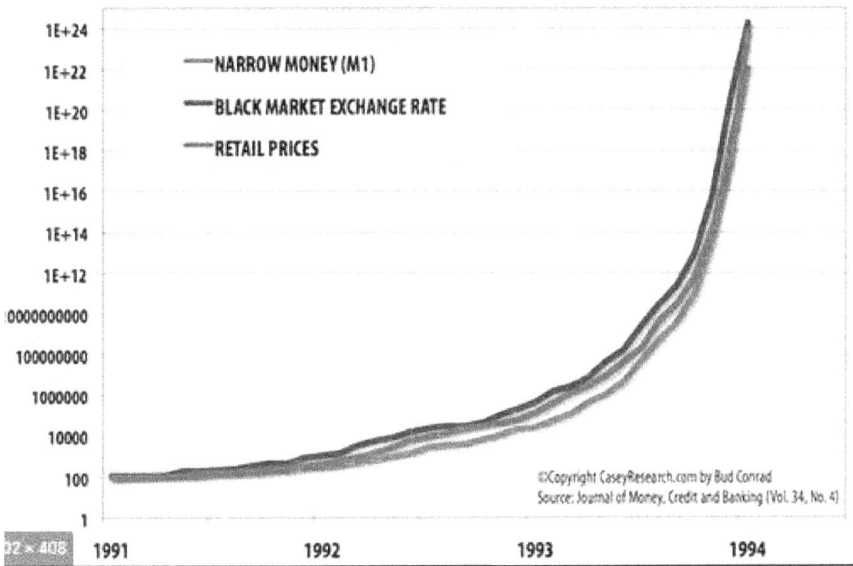

Source: (Watkins, 2010).

The Federal Republic of Yugoslavia (FRY) ranks among the nations that have experienced the worst financial crisis in history. FRY had one of the most extended periods of hyperinflation that lasted from 1992 to 1994. During this 2-year-period, the nation recorded an inflation rate of 313,000,000% each month. The daily inflation was more than 62%, making the situation more dire than in the Weimar

Republic (Hanke, 2007). Like other regions that have been unfortunate to experience economic devastation, political instability and poor decision-making on monetary and fiscal policies are often at the center of the crisis. This chapter will reveal an in-depth analysis of the contributing factors, the impact hyperinflation had on society, and the mitigation plans implemented to curb further prices. According to Hanke (2007), the virulent nature of the financial crisis in Yugoslavia in the 1990s made it stand out from other countries that grappled with hyperinflation. The country's highest recorded inflation rate at the peak of the financial crisis was 313 million percent (Watkins, 2010). This made it second to the Hungarian hyperinflation that occurred in the 1940s.

The Leadup

The causes and origin of the economic problems have been traced back to the Tito regime when the government embarked on a mission to address budget deficits by authorizing the printing of more money. This marked the beginning of implementing an irrational economic decision that increased the reliance on printing money to finance government operations and boost economic growth. The Communist Party took over the reins of power after the Tito administration adopted the same irrational policies as its predecessors. The Yugoslav government had depleted most of the currency reserves and imposed restrictions on private citizens. This made it easier for the authorities to access the hard currency reserves of private individuals stored in the commercial banks. The nation's inflation rate increased by almost 25% annually from the 1970s to the years leading up to the hyperinflation. In the early 1990s, it was discovered that the Serbian National Bank, under the instructions of Slobodan Milosevic, had issued more than $1.4 billion credit to his friends (Petrović, Bogetić & Vujošević, 1999). The amount was approximately half of what the National Bank of Yugoslavia intended to pump into the economy. This created deficits for the Markovic regime, making it impossible for the government to support economic growth.

Figure 2. *Aftermath of the of Croatia and Bosnia–Herzegovina war.*

Source: (Taylor, 2012).

Milosevic's heist sabotaged the new regime and escalated the divisive politics in the region. This culminated in Slovenia and Croatia breaking away from the Socialist Federal Republic of Yugoslavia. The disintegration from the former SFRY resulted in political and social unrest in the region. War broke out in Croatia and Bosnia-Herzegovina in 1992, which saw the monthly inflation rate surpass the 50% mark (Taylor, 2012). The newly formed Federal Republic of Yugoslavia

(FRY) was on the verge of a severe financial crisis and total destruction as Figure 2 depicts. The dissolution of the SFRY had far-reaching economic impacts on the region. This political impasse had disrupted regional trade that adversely affected the production level of most industries. The government expense increased due to war and the payment of civil servants. The military and police force of the former SFRY remained in Serbia and Montenegro, which was a smaller territory creating a burden on the region's government expenditure. The administration in SFRY was fighting against all odds to prevent a decline in economic growth, which resulted in the incorporation of irrational policies that escalated the crisis.

The collapse of the stabilization programs implemented by the Yugoslav government also played a vital role in escalating the county's inflation rates. At the beginning of 1989, Markovic's regime had embarked on creating policies aimed at the opening up the nation's economy (Taylor, 2012). This comprised placing bans on both economic and political blockades to stimulate economic growth. Although the stabilization programs effectively solved the country's financial problems, they were only short-term solutions that could not address the high inflation rates. The economy was already showing inflation, and any programs to boost the economy failed to bear the desired results.

First signs and the hyperinflation years

Since the first signs of inflation were discovered in Yugoslavia, the inflationary period had shown an uncontrollable increase in commodity prices. The inflation rate peaked rapidly within the two years, with the highest record being witnessed in 1994 (He, 2017). After the region declared *de facto* trading, activities were adversely affected, with many industries experiencing a decline in total output. The war in Croatia and Bosnia–Herzegovina jeopardized security in the region and made the economic situation worse. The 1990s for Yugoslavia was a period of persistent hardship, creating a slippery slope scenario whereby one problem led to the other (He, 2017). During this time, the United Nations imposed sanctions and trade embargos on international transactions with the Federal Republic of Yugoslavia. The sanctions by the United Nations escalated the decline in output and the productivity

of the economy. Following this, the government authorized the printing

of more money to boost the purchasing power of the citizens.

Figure 3. *Banknote denomination of RSD 500,000,000,000.*

Source: ((Watkins, 2010)

The government mint was working overtime to supply more

money in circulation. It is estimated that it was producing nearly nine

hundred thousand notes each month. For instance, the Topčider mint

started making high denomination banknotes such as the RSD

500,000,000,000 as shown in figure 3. The only problem was that by the time the money was getting in the hands of the citizens, it was already worthless because of the high devaluation of the dinar. This eventually led to the collapse of the national currency forcing the public to adopt the German Mark as the accepted legal tender. The citizens relied on the black-market exchange rate to convert the dinar to the German Mark. The Yugoslav foreign exchange reserve declined as the value of the dinar dropped against other foreign currencies. The public was starving because of a shortage in commodities, and the high price tags made it difficult for them to afford products in the free market. Milosevic blamed the country's misfortune on external forces such as the trade embargos initiated by the United Nations (He, 2017). His administration spent most of the printed money to finance the war between Croatia and Bosnia–Herzegovina. Gasoline became a rare commodity in Belgrade, and most people were forced to cease driving (He, 2017). Only government officials and embassy personnel could access the gas from the only station that remained operational.

Sanctions against the FR of Yugoslavia were enforced on 30 May 1992, by the United Nations Security Council on charges of contributing to the conflict in Bosnia and Herzegovina. The UN Security Council goal accommodated a total global financial ban on this country. Affected by worldwide sanctions, there was a significant financial emergency in the country and the development of hyperinflation, which likewise saw the issuance of a banknote with a record division of RSD 500,000,000,000 (Stojković, 2019).

From 1992, the Yugoslav dinar encountered a hyperinflation that went on for 25 months. Prices rose quickly, such that in late 1992 and early 1993 inflation exploded, taking on practically unfathomable extents. During 1993 prices went up by 116.5 thousand billion percent, and in the initial three weeks of 1994 by 313 million percent (He, 2017). The force of hyperinflation recorded in late 1993 and mid-1994, the FR Yugoslavia is among the worst (Stojković, 2019) ever recorded in history.

Consumer Behavior

Consumers were the most affected as prices of goods and services skyrocketed overnight. For a long time, essential stores and gas stations remain closed except for one station that served embassies and other foreign personnel. Many people turned to the black market to trade huge amounts of worthless dinars for the US dollar or the German mark note. Between 1991 and 1998, the dinar was devalued more than eighteen times. The country's monetary orgy ended when the Topcider mint became incapacitated because it was converting 500-billion-dinar bills into insignificant change, which caused the machine's ink to dry out.

The Deleveraging and Stabilization

Yugoslavia applied two currency stabilization programs: heterodox and orthodox. The heterodox approach was adopted at the culmination of the socialist federal republic (SFRY) while the orthodox approach was applied at the commencement of the Federal Republic of

Yugoslavia (FRY). Both measures were relatively effective in the short-

term but remained unsuccessful in the long-term, which led to their

collapse. The initial program was implemented in the 1980s as an

economic reform program. However, by 1994, another program –

monetary reconstruction program and economic recovery (also known

as the 'Avramović Program'), was implemented.

This prompted a destruction of the domestic economy, as fares

become financially impossible, and imports are extremely rewarding.

Remembering that there has been an advancement of imports, the

domestic market is "overpowered" with imported items, which are

consumed by expanding domestic interest, only for consumer

merchandise powered by quick compensation development

(Cunningham et al, 2011). Imports of merchandise become less

expensive than domestic ones, so there is a decrease in production

because our items are not backed by anything solid. After a few stretches of execution, modern production was decreased by 25%, and unemployment expanded by 18% (He, 2017).

The second, long-term stage involved fundamental monetary changes that (while saving the dependability accomplished in the primary stage) would prompt the financial recuperation of the country. This would guarantee long-term stable financial development with an ideal work rate and the development of residents' norms. This stage, as the creators of the program have brought up, expected the nullification of financial approvals and the progression of "new" capital required for its development. Since this was not accomplished, this subsequent stage got no opportunity for significant achievement, similar to the case with the primary period of the Program (He, 2017).

North Korea Hyperinflation

Introduction

In a meeting with the International Monetary Fund (IMF)
delegates in 1997, North Korean representatives provided some data
that showed that the GDP of their country had fallen by half in the
preceding four years and that the condition of the economy was
deteriorating. North Korea's request to join the IMF has never been
approved because of the nation's political hurdles. The North Korean
government has no practice releasing statistics often, and most of the
economic data regarding the country has been grounded on third-party
estimates.

For years, the North Korean economy has suffered due to low
manufacturing production. In recent years, the country's crippling
economy has been exacerbated by harsh, international economic
sanctions because of North Korea's regime and nuclear programs (He,
2017). With the death of the supreme leader Kim Jong-il in 2011, the

international community hoped that his successor would launch constructive economic and political reforms. However, one year after taking power, the new leader had not delivered his promised economic reforms, and the country's economy continued to crumble. In the last decade, North Korea has faced international criticism because of its domestic nuclear program. However, this distracted the world from the nation's economic woes at the start of the decade.

For years, the North Korean currency, the Won, has been officially secured by the USD. As such, exchange controls and many connected regulations and punitive penalties have rendered the won inconvertible. A robust black market for foreign currency has risen in the country (Powell, 2009). This has resulted in severe inflationary consequences.

Lead up to Hyperinflation

The pertinent question is, how can hyperinflation happen in an economy where the government controls almost every aspect of the nation, from prices of goods to local and foreign trade? Ordinary

148

individuals in North Korea are allocated essential supplies of food, health care, housing, and education for free but in limited quantities. Since the late 1990s, after an era of economic inaction and natural calamities that led to famine, North Korea relaxed government controls by allowing private business on a small scale while looking for a Stalinist-styled financial system. Numerous joint ventures with overseas companies from South Korea and other nations developed in North Korea in recent years. Tourism has become a crucial source of foreign exchange. Consequently, a shadow economy has been growing in the nation.

A state can exercise monetary policy as long as the nation's household sector holds a considerable amount of money. And this is what occurred in North Korea at the start of the 21st century. Just like South Korea, North Korea has used a currency system since the 1940s. From the 1940s, the nation has experienced four primary currency reforms in 1959, 1979, 1992, and 2009. In each reform, old notes were withdrawn quickly, and new notes with larger denominations were issued (Powell, 2009). The 1959 and 2009 reforms included redenomination as new notes replaced old notes at a rate of 100 to 1. As a result, these forms mandated the cancelation of excess currency held by its citizens and caused an expansionary monetary policy. Additionally, money stock in the country has been expanding at a faster rate than inhibited inflation.

In the late 1900s, as new international revenues started to flow into North Korea, the state attempted to rebuild the image of its socialist economy. In 2000, North Koreans held around $964 million in foreign exchange, with an average of $186 per household, of which 60% was in USD, and the rest was primarily in Chinese Renminbi (Powell, 2009). The foreign exchange reserves allowed the country to import luxury commodities or save money with stable value. There are stores in North Korea where one could only purchase using foreign currency like the USD, the Chinese Renminbi, and the Japanese Yen. The exchange rates on the black market differed significantly from the state's rates (Powell, 2009).

First Sign of Hyperinflation

However, these efforts mainly took the form of initiatives intended to strengthen central planning. In 2002, the state suddenly instituted a wide range of economic measures. Here, the government downsized official ration guarantees, increased wages, and consumption prices drastically, and dramatically slashed the official exchange rate (Eberstadt, 2010). As a result, these initiatives increased the sanctioned function of currency and markets. In 2003, the North Korean regime undertook a public bond for an unstipulated amount. The bonds had a ten-year maturity with no fixed interest rate (Eberstadt, 2010). Bondholders were compensated with a lottery-grounded cash prize.

However, these economic measures failed to work as intended. Consequently, there was a lot of new money circulating in the economy, generating significant inflation. By November 2009, the North Korean won's black-market value in dollars was hardly 5% of the level when the 2002 measures were implemented, a depreciation averaging over 3% per month (Eberstadt, 2010). Here, the North

Korean government attempted to tackle these problems with a single

swift blow with the currency reform of 2009.

Hyperinflation Years

In November 2009, the North Korean government instituted a

currency reform. There were two main reasons for the 2009 currency

reform. First, North Korea was experiencing a widening gap between

the rich and the poor because of the relatively free markets (Powell,

2009). The state felt that the currency change would reduce inequality

by making a broad swath of its population poorer. However, the gap

continued to persist since the most prominent and wealthiest merchants,

including state-owned companies, had long swapped the North Korean

won and instead held the Chinese Yuan and the USD as a store of

value. The black market value of the won has been decreasing for years,

and North Korean inflation has been accelerating. Secondly, the

government wanted control of the economy (Powell, 2009). The state

allowed the black market to grow out of desperation, but it had

expanded to a point where the government felt threatened. Small merchants and black markets existed outside state control, and the regime could not allow this to continue. Hence, the reform was intended to deal a significant blow to black markets and enable the state to tighten its control of the economy.

The 2009 currency reform was a catastrophic initiative for North Korea. The state attempted to handle runaway inflation by instituting a deceptive currency initiative (He, 2017). In reality, the reform was a currency redenomination program that arbitrarily eliminated two zeros off every note. The residents were given less than two weeks to exchange all their won for new currency notes. The state set limits on the amount of won a household could exchange for new won. In December 2009, the government established the redenomination at a rate of 1 new note for 100 old notes (He, 2017). There were maximum restrictions for each household in the exchange.

The state extended upper limits to individuals' bank deposits. For those who had saved a lot of won, the reform acted as an effective wealth tax initiative. Individuals with savings of more than the maximum allowed for exchange were at risk of losing their savings.

The government did not make a public announcement about the 2009 currency reform. Instead, it used internal channels, including cable radio and loudspeakers in local communities, to notify the people about the currency conversion. The state asserted that the purpose of the currency reform was to prevent inflation, limit the black markets, and readjust the economic system. However, this caused widespread panic and chaos in North Korea. As a result, people rushed to rural areas to purchase rice and corn, and others flooded the black market to buy foreign currency, which plummeted the won, as shown in Figure 1. Individuals holding foreign currency lined at the doors of stores that sold goods in foreign exchange.

Figure 1. *The price of rice*

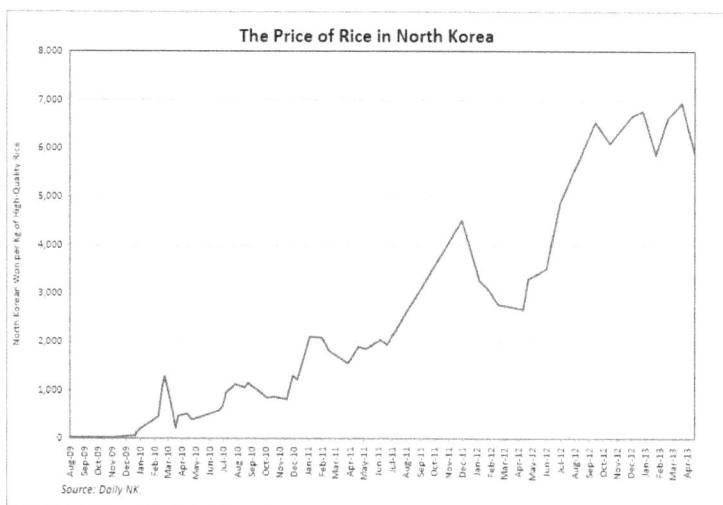

Source: (Hanke, S. (2013)

The state had to delay the currency conversion for a day, and it closed all stores and department stores for three days. It sent armed police to the streets to maintain order in cities. In February 2010, the state decided to relax the limitations to prevent more protests and revolts from the residents (He, 2017). Owing to redenomination, the value of the won against the dollar collapsed, and the price of essential commodities skyrocketed. Within two months, prices of rice and corn soared in the countryside. Rice prices doubled within the first two

weeks of December. As the won plunged, inflation surged. North Korea

officially entered hyperinflation in December 2009 as inflation

exceeded 50% per month. The hyperinflation reached its peak in March

2010, when the monthly inflation rate reached 926%. At the same time,

prices rose 28.5 times between December 2009 and March 2010 (He,

2017).

Figure 2. *The fall of the won.*

The Fall in the Value of the North Korean Won
The Black-Market North Korean Won/U.S. Dollar Exchange Rate

Source: (Hanke, S. (2013)

In March 2010, the North Korean government tried to stop inflation but bore little success. Hyperinflation gradually continued to affect the nation, as depicted in figure 3. Black market exchange rates remained considerably higher than the state's rates. Due to the country's nuclear program, its trade flows were increasingly restricted by the United Nations. Consequently, North Korea remained isolated, which increased its foreign exchange scarcity, severely affecting its economy. To address the budget deficit that emerged because of a stagnant economy and isolation from the global economy, North Korea embarked on monetary policy to sustain its economy and manage inflation. It was not until January 2011 that North Korea's hyperinflation came to an end (Hanke, 2013).

Figure 3. *Monthly inflation rate*

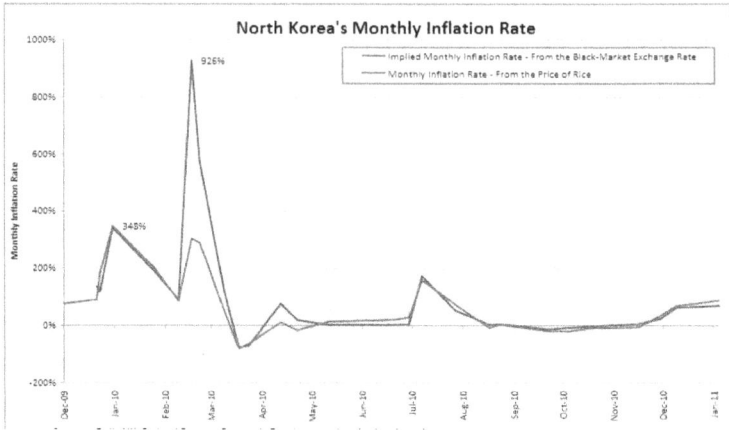

Source: (Hanke, 2013)

Consumer Impact

The reform sparked a panic in the country's underground

markets for goods and services. The black markets, which emerged out

of necessity during the famine of the 1990s, mainly existed to

counteract shortages that emerged because of government control of

agriculture (Hanke, 2013). According to the United Nations, almost half

of the food consumed by North Koreans was bought in these black

markets. Due to the bungled currency reform, the demand for hard

158

currency (USD and Chinese Yuan) skyrocketed as more and more

traders in the black markets required transactions to occur in hard cash.

Consequently, the value of the won tumbled on the black market.

During the hyperinflation era, many North Koreans started to exchange

their depreciating won for more stable foreign currencies like the USD

and the Chinese Yuan to preserve their savings and purchasing power.

The Deleveraging

In 2011, Kim Jong-un assumed power to inherit an economy

that looked like a disaster. The new leader instantaneously instituted

policies to stabilize the currency, prices, and the entire economy.

Instead of enacting another devastating currency reform, the new leader

embarked on a two-pronged monetary approach. First, he changed the

domestic monetary policy to shadow the USD on the black market

(Hanke, 2013). The Won/USD exchange rate stability became the

Nation's primary monetary goal. Second, the government introduced a

policy of benign neglect that facilitated the spontaneous dollarization of

the North Korean economy (Hanke, 2013). As a result, the Chinese

Yuan and the USD became the economy's currency in practice, replacing the KPW.

The new leader also allowed the black market economy to thrive. He made it possible for vast parts of the economy to privatize impulsively. As the effects of the international sanctions started to affect North Korea, the state developed various squeeze-avoidance strategies.

North Korea embarked on a dollarization approach to address the hyperinflation, as the method has been used by other inflation-ravaged nations, like Zimbabwe and Venezuela. (In June 2008, Zimbabwe's hyperinflation reached a yearly rate of 89.7 sextillion percent (Hanke, 2013). As a result, the people abandoned the Zimbabwe dollar and exclusively utilized the USD and other stable currencies, like the South African Rand and the Mozambican metical. Zimbabwe's hyperinflation stopped instantaneously, and the inflation rates returned to single digits. Due to the dollarization of the economy, Zimbabwe's government was mandated to accept the end of the Zimbabwe dollar and legitimately dollarize the economy).

Since 2011, the Chinese Yuan and the USD have been used more widely in North Korea than the won. Based on recent statistics, North Korean markets along the Chinese border conduct about 80% of their transactions in the Chinese Yuan (Hanke, 2013). Similarly, merchants inside the country conducted about 50% of their transactions in USD. This trend was a result of spontaneous dollarization. The practice of dumping the local currency in favor of stable foreign currency became widespread despite the government criminalizing the circulation of foreign currencies on the black markets.

An excellent example is Kaesong Industrial Complex, which was jointly owned by North and South Korea (Hanke, 2013). Employees utilized a South Korean marshmallow cookie treat, called the ChocoPie, as an unofficial currency within the complex. The USD exchange rate for a ChocoPie reached close to $10 in Kaesong before the administration stopped providing its employees their bonuses in ChocoPies (Hanke, 2013).

Although the North Korean government did not allow foreign currency, spontaneous dollarization was and is a reality, especially along the Chinese border. There were calls for North Korea to Yuan-ize its economy since China accounts for more than 50% of North Korea's foreign trade and a vast share of its foreign direct investment (Hanke, 2013). Since the mid-2000s, China has continued to increase its trade and investments in North Korea, especially along the border. China is also working to build infrastructure, such as bridges, power links, and high-speed rail lines in the Northeast (Hanke, 2013). Therefore, the official adoption of the Yuan by North Korea would end the inflation woes and facilitate increased trade with China and neighboring nations.

Consequently, such action would counter the current US policy stance against North Korea. However, North Korea has shown it is not affected by the sanctions placed by the international community since it is willing to let its people starve while it pursues nuclear capabilities. For China, yuan-ization and economic reforms in North Korea would result in a much less combative and dangerous neighbor. This is why China is pushing for increased integration of China's Northeast region and North Korea.

Kim Jong-un's spontaneous dollarization and privatization strategies have worked in reducing inflation and stimulating the North Korean economy. Today, the won has stabilized against other currencies in the foreign exchange since 2012. Additionally, the prices of essential commodities, such as rice, have been stable since 2012. This shows that North Korea is not haunted by inflation anymore. Today, the black market has become the new normal. Kim Jong-Un's government has little choice but to continue its fledgling efforts at economic reforms that reflect market realities on the ground or risk losing its grip on power (Pearson, 2015).

Bonus

As you are probably used to not getting enough for your money in an inflationary environment, we've decided to buck the trend and actually give you an extra example of HyperInflation – The recent HyperInflation in Zimbabwe under Robert Mughabe.

Hyperinflation in Zimbabwe

Zimbabwe's hyperinflation story is one of the worst in recent history. It's a story of mismanagement and corruption. Zimbabwe had always been plagued by high inflation. Zimbabwe had rates of inflation around 10% in the 1980's and 1990's. It started spiking in 2000 and reached 100% in 2001. From 2006, the inflation rate rose to over 1500% annually and by September that year, it entered an extended period of hyperinflation. By the year 2009, Zimbabwe was experiencing record hyperinflation of over 80 billion percent every month. By January the same year, the country had experienced a decade of high inflation above 100% every year since 2001 (Matiashe, 2021). As of 2018, inflation in Zimbabwe rose to 10% and jumped dramatically to 622% in 2020 as shown in figure 1.

Figure 1. *Zimbabwe inflation rate from 1985-2025*

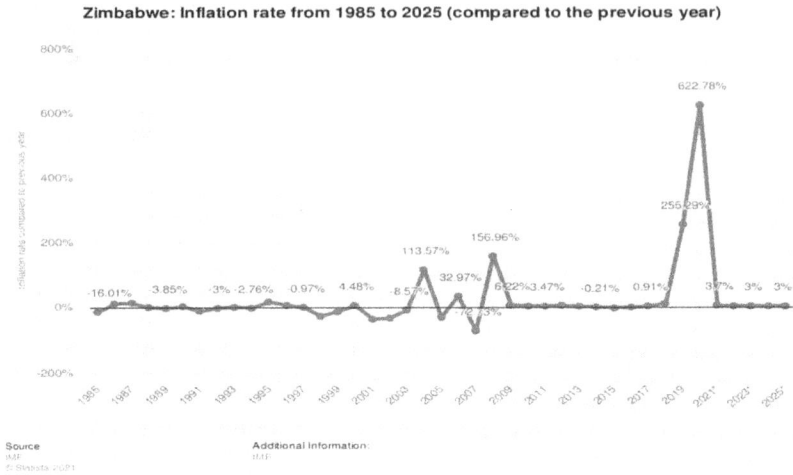

Source: (O'Neill, 2021).

The financial crisis in Zimbabwe was caused by a combination

of factors. These causes were linked to poor governance and

establishment of inappropriate polices. The Zimbabwean land reforms

during Mugabe's regime are an excellent example of poor decision-

making that exacerbated the effects of the hyperinflation. In the early

2000s, Mugabe orchestrated a paramilitary mission that involved the

seizure of more than 23 million acres from commercial owners and

166

foreigners (Matiashe, 2021). The objective here was to shift ownership of the property rights to the local population. The confiscated land was given to would-be farmers who lacked knowledge on commercial farming. This was a huge blow to the agricultural sector, which was the country's biggest source of revenue. When the new landowners failed to handle commercial production, they went back to subsistence farming causing a shortage in food production. The ripple effect of the land seizure also had a detrimental impact on food processing companies and exporters that eventually shut down their operations.

The Lead up to Hyperinflation in Zimbabwe

To understand the reasons behind Zimbabwe's hyperinflation, it is important to have a look at the skewed land reforms, corruption and misguided policies. The initial impetus to Zimbabwe's Road to hyperinflation was from unwise fiscal policies needed to pacify populist groups. This worsened the situation as influential people wanted resources for free (Kairiza, 2012). These resources were being taken from foreign investors with property in the country and handed over to local citizens.

With corruption rife, political and influential figures in the government grabbed majority of the lucrative resources. The move caused investors to exit the country and refrain from trading with the Zimbabwean currency. This resulted in depreciation and cost-push inflation. The subsequent fall in production that accompanied the set land reforms and resultant turbulences in the agricultural sector further worsened the situation. In addition, the central bank was compromised by the ruling party, since it was getting funds from state coffers to amass wealth and influence.

Robert Mugabe's rhetoric on confiscating white-owned land was elevated in the 2000s when war veterans assumed prominent seats in the ruling ZANU PF party. As a result, the country's agricultural output fell from 18% of GDP in 2000 to 14% in 2002 (World Bank, 2008). Tobacco, which is one of Zimbabwe's top foreign exchange earners was also greatly affected, as shown in Figure 2. Export proceeds from tobacco fell from $612 million in 1999 to $321 million in 2003.

Failing agricultural output meant that the government could no longer

service its debt obligations, which prompted the international financial

institutions to suspend further lending to the country.

Figure 2. *Tobacco output (in millions of Dollars) from 1999-2004*

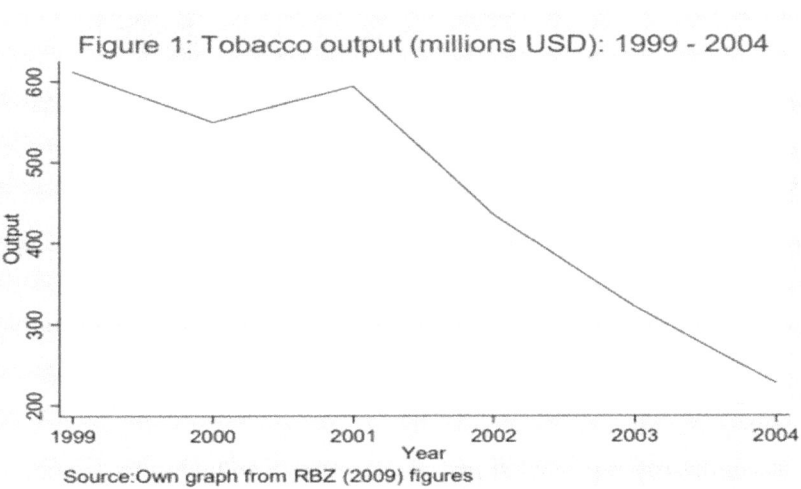

Figure 1: Tobacco output (millions USD): 1999 - 2004

Source: (Reserve Bank of Zimbabwe RBZ, 2021)

By 2008, the country had the second-highest hyperinflation rate

in the world which stood at 79 billion percent by November that year.

The daily inflation rate was 98%. Prices for all commodities doubled every new day and there was an unemployment rate of 80%. In a bid to save the country from complete ruin, the government became desperate and begun to overprint money in response to the economic shocks.

The First Signs of Hyperinflation

After independence, Zimbabwean authorities launched economic reforms to liberalize the economy and deal with structural barriers to growth. However, the same was done with weak fiscal and monetary policies in place. In early 1999, the actions led to a scale-back of assistance from foreign donors and financial institutions (Coomer and Gstraunthaler, 2011). Concisely, by the new millennium, the country's economy had turned precarious. Inflation began to accelerate after mid-2001 when government borrowing advanced towards the statutory limit set at 20% of the previous year's earnings. Despite this, the government blamed it on avaricious profiteering as opposed to a result of the RBZ's weak monetary policies. Economic deterioration and the road towards hyperinflation began in the first five months of 2005. Annual inflation rates stabilized to 135% in early 2005 and shot up to 164% by June. This mirrored the slackening of monetary policy and decline in foreign exchange. Coomer and Gstraunthaler (2011) state that by 2006, interest rates remained deeply negative with exchange rates against the US dollar sitting at 135,000 Zimbabwean dollars to one US dollar. The money market returns were elevated and the RBZ introduced index-linked, single-yield treasury bills. Figure 3 below shows a 100 trillion-dollar note printed by the Zimbabwean Reserve Bank.

Figure 3. *One hundred trillion dollar note from Zimbabwe*

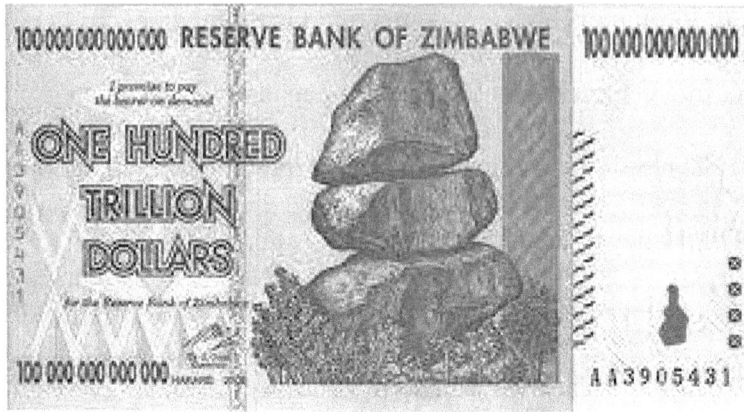

Source: (Pettinger, 2019)

Zimbabwe officially entered hyperinflation – reaching an annual

rate of 2200% and a monthly rate of 50.54% - in March 2007

(Coomber, 2010). Throughout the rest of 2007, Zimbabwe's

manufacturing output declined by over 50% (Dewa et al, 2013). Once

the inflation rate shot over the threshold of hyperinflation, the erosion

of the country's tax base deteriorated. By May 2009, the annual

inflation rate surpassed 1000%. Monetary supply figures for that year

indicated that the growth rate stood at over 1400%.

By 2008, hyperinflation had begun gaining momentum hitting over 400000% in March. In December the same year, the foreign currency used as a medium of exchange was rendered useless, unofficially. This marked the initial unsanctioned dollarization in Zimbabwe. As of January 2009, the finance minister authorized the legal use of the US dollar and the SA Rand thus affirming official dollarization (Kairiza, 2012). Hyperinflation continued being fueled by weak quasi-fiscal activities that culminated in a swift increase in bank deposits with the reserve bank thereby increasing local currency. As Coomer and Gstraunthaler (2011) illustrate, by the end of 2008, reserve money fell from USD 7 million to an exchange rate of 35 quadrillion Zimbabwean dollars per one US dollar.

The Hyperinflation Years

Towards the end of 2008, Zimbabwe was undergoing one of the worst hyperinflation rates in history. According to the Economic Times (2008), a loaf of bread cost the equivalent of twelve new cars whereas a packet of locally-produced coffee cost 1 billion Zimbabwean dollars. At the peak of hyperinflation, commodity prices doubled daily.

Commodities like gasoline had to be traded in US dollars or SA Rands

and barter trade became common. Zimbabwean currency became

almost worthless as shown in Figure 4 below.

Figure 4. *Zimbabweans out crying over the hyperinflation*

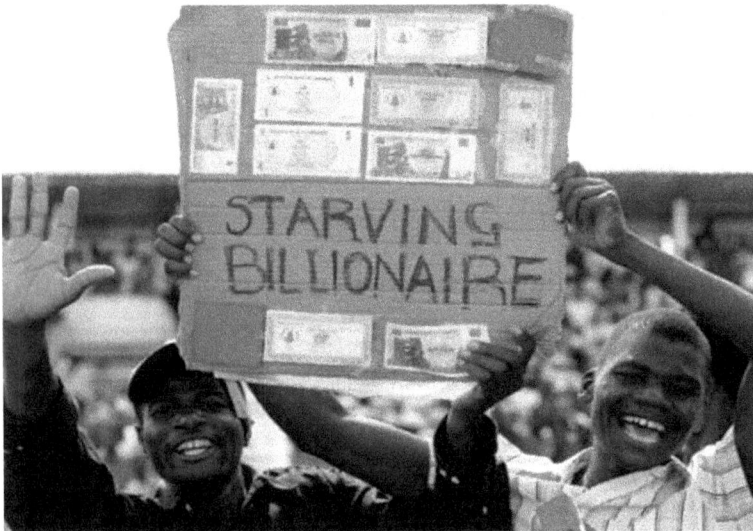

Source: (*mhseconomics*, 2016)

As mentioned earlier, the hyperinflation in Zimbabwe did not occur overnight and was the product of a prolonged decline in the country's economic growth. The unprecedented market forces had adversely affected the economy leading to economic stagnation. Sources revealed that the agricultural and manufacturing sectors were failing long before the outbreak of the financial crisis. The country was also facing an increase in the national debt that became a hefty burden for the taxpayers. With reduced productivity, the economy exhibited a downward spiral that perpetuated the inflationary period. The government, too, played a significant role in exacerbating the situation, by implementing inappropriate policy reforms that caused a decline in economic growth. All the factors that led to hyperinflation seem to be correlated and culminated in severe consequences to the public.

Assessing the level of inflation in Zimbabwe is complex given that the government deliberately failed to post inflation statistics. However, using Cagan's definition of hyperinflation, the conclusion is that the country began to experience hyperinflation in February 2007.

The height of the hyperinflation was in November 2008 as shown in

Figure 5.

Figure 5. *Zimbabwe's official hyperinflation rate 1980-2008*

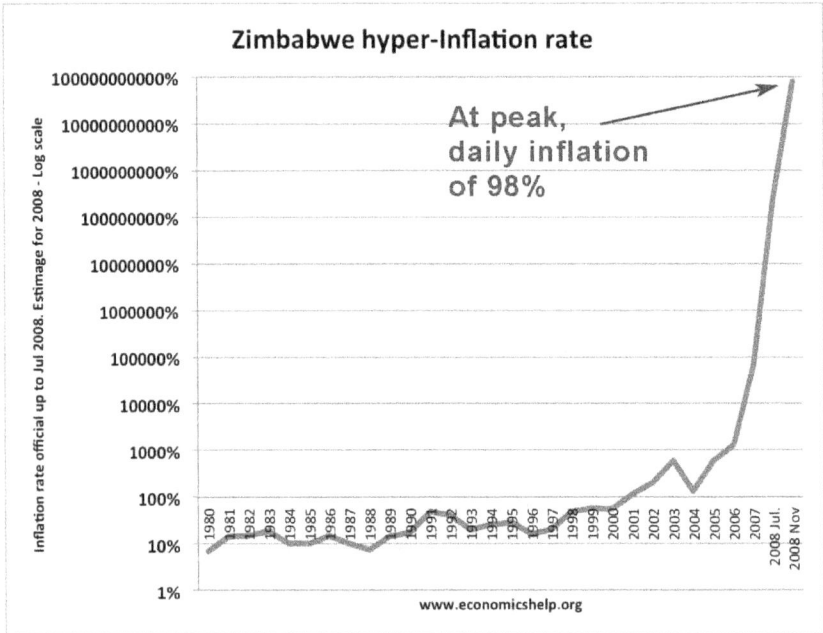

Source: (Pettinger, 2019).

Consumer Behavior during the Inflationary Period

One of the noteworthy effects of hyperinflation in Zimbabwe is

that it eroded the consumer's purchasing power. According to the law of

demand, an increase in the price of commodities causes a decline in the

public's ability to purchase commodities. Hyperinflation is

characterized by a prolonged period of more than a 50% rise in the

market's cost of goods and services. As a result, it becomes daunting for

the consumer to afford basic needs such as food, shelter and clothing.

This was the situation in Zimbabwe during the inflationary period.

According to Conkling (2010), the price for commodities was

increasing at a higher rate than the income and wages of the consumers.

Since the income level did not keep pace with the country's inflation,

most Zimbabweans couldn't afford basic items such as bread and milk.

The cost of living, particularly for those residing in urban areas like

Harare, became too much for ordinary people to bear (Conkling, 2010).

This implied that urban residents and those who had relocated to the

city for employment had to compensate and forego luxuries to thrive

and survive the financial crisis. The progression of the challenging economic times culminated in a scenario whereby the citizens experienced prices doubling every day. For instance, a loaf of bread would cost twice as much today as it was yesterday. Such hiked prices of essential commodities hit the media by storm and cast a spotlight on the country's failing economy.

The government responded by printing more money to offset national debt and cushion the economic shocks the country encountered at the time. This money creation approach adopted by the government aimed to reassure the public and improve people's faith in the government. Consumers lost their confidence in the Zimbabwean dollar, devaluing rapidly against other currencies. For instance, people required millions to purchase essential commodities like bread. According to Baldauf (2008), the average price of a loaf of bread during the inflationary period was approximately 10 million Zimbabwe dollars. The consumers were forced to embrace the use of foreign currencies when purchasing goods and commodities. When the government refrained from further printing money, the people relied on currencies such as the Rand and the American dollar as the accepted medium of exchange.

Inflation was officially declared illegal in 2007 by the government to prevent further increases in prices. This permitted arrests of any businessmen who hiked the prices of goods and services in the Zimbabwean market. Implementing price controls only resulted in more financial problems for the country, instead of stopping inflation. The government's attempts to regulate prices in the economy, coupled with the inability of the agricultural sector to supply food, led to massive shortages. Productivity had dwindled, and business entities had to import foreign commodities to sell to the consumers. The use of foreign currency made it easier for such individuals to import commodities and engage in daily transactions with consumers. For consumers, they needed to switch to other currencies because retaining the Zimbabwe dollar was cumbersome. People were forced to use millions to purchase simple items like bread and milk (Baldauf, 2008).

The government was compelled to adopt the multi-currency system to sustain businesses and other economic activities. Local shops were established in a bid to enable the citizenry to buy foreign currency. However, the demand for foreign currency facilitated by the multi-currency system attracted the attention of the black market. A shadow market existed outside the legal space that provided currency exchange services for citizens who needed to convert their Zimbabwe dollars before it dropped in value. Additionally, the black market provided certain commodities consumed daily by the households in the region. The low productivity in Zimbabwe created a shortage of daily consumables like bread, soap, and in extreme cases, groceries. The people were going through hard times that made life in the country unbearable. The transportation sector was among the industries that were worst affected during the inflationary period. Commuters and bus drivers had to deal with the unprecedented changes in oil prices and currency exchange.

Most of the foreigners living in the region fled the financial crisis. Zimbabwe had received sanctions from the international community that made the region unattractive for foreign investment. The unemployment rate during the economic crisis had reached a record-high of over 70% (Conkling, 2010). With most citizens rendered

jobless, the income level couldn't keep up with the inflation.

Additionally, the manufacturing and agricultural sectors were

underperforming, causing some of the companies to shut down. The

high unemployment in the country subjected most of the families in

Harare and other areas to abject poverty. The hoarding of perishable

commodities was also witnessed among consumers and suppliers. As

the money in the economy lost value, people opted for barter trade,

where commodities were exchanged for other services and goods. The

economy later switched to the American dollar to salvage business

activities and prevent further financial problems.

Deleveraging

As mentioned earlier, poor decision-making by the government

played a crucial role in exacerbating the inflation. The devaluing of the

Zimbabwe dollar had far-reaching consequences. The only feasible

solution for the economy was adopting a foreign currency. This led to

the demonetization that allowed the switch to the American dollar in

2015 (Conkling, 2010). Since then, most of the transactions in the country were in either American dollars or the South African Rand. The new regime that took the reins of power after Mugabe was ousted, outlawed the use of foreign currency. The decision saw the creation of a new local currency. Despite this, the country is on the verge of another financial crisis, with reports that the price for commodities has increased over the past half-decade. Zimbabwe is yet to fully recover from the 2008 hyperinflation, and citizens face challenges coping with the current economic situation. The International Monetary Fund has ranked Zimbabwe second to Venezuela for having the highest current inflation levels in the world.

Conclusion

Hyperinflation is a rarity in an economy. As discussed in the different cases of extreme inflation in this book, hyperinflation is detrimental to countries. While hyperinflation has become an increasingly popular topic today, few people around the globe understand the toll it has on the common man and the future of generations to come. The subject has become popular because similar situations that later lead to hyperinflation are being witnessed today. Hyperinflation presents governments with circumstances that render them helpless. The various instances of hyperinflation discussed in this book open the lid to a comparable pattern of governments becoming desperate and introducing policies that worsen the inflation problem. Most hyperinflations have a catalyst. The catalyst can be an external shock, such as war, famine, or a pandemic; or internal mismanagement of resources. The trigger causes mild to moderate inflation that starts damaging the economy. The Government panics and starts printing money to fix economic problems. This creates more inflation and further craters the economy, making the Government print even more. This cycle continues till hyperinflation. It's comparable to a person addicted to heroin. The person needs a little heroine at first to feel good and forget about the problems in life. Once the high wears off, he feels terrible at having to return to everyday life. He again takes the same amount of the drug. Since his body has adapted to that amount of the drug, he needs even more heroin to get the same high. And this cycle continues till the person dies or goes into rehab.

Governments that have independent central banks rarely experience extreme cases of hyperinflation, as they are quick to remove the fiscal stimulus. In retrospect, enhancing the independence of a country's central bank helps a country evade the menace of hyperinflation.

The end... almost!

Reviews are not easy to come by.

As an independent author with a tiny marketing budget, I rely on readers, like you, to leave a short review on Amazon.

Even if it's just a sentence or two!

So, if you enjoyed the book, please...

>> Click here to leave a brief review on Amazon.

I am very appreciative for your review as it truly makes a difference.

Thank you from the bottom of my heart for purchasing this book and reading it to the end.

References

Intro

Toscano, P. (2014). The Worst Hyperinflation Situations of All Time.

Retrieved 31 May 2021, from

https://www.cnbc.com/2011/02/14/The-Worst-Hyperinflation-

Situations-of-All-Time.html

Civil War HyperInflation

Doyle, B. G. (2001). Hyperinflation and the confederacy: an

interdisciplinary lesson in economics and history. *Social*

Education, *65*(6), 366-373.

Lerner, E (1955). "Money, Prices, and Wages in the Confederacy:

1861-1865," *Journal of Political Economy* 63: 20-40.

Library of Congress (n.d). *Confederate flag flying.*

https://www.loc.gov/resource/ppmsca.32284/

Rhodes, J. F., & Long, E. B. (1999). *History of the civil war, 1861-*

1865. Courier Corporation.

U.S. Department of Commerce (1949). *Historical Statistics of the United States 1789-1945.* [PDF]. https://www2.census.gov/prod2/statcomp/documents/Historical StatisticsoftheUnitedStates1789-1945.pdf

Inflation and hyper definition

Amadeo, K. (2020). Could You Survive Hyperinflation?. Retrieved 31 May 2021, from https://www.thebalance.com/what-is-hyperinflation-definition-causes-and-examples-3306097

Salemi, M. (2021). Hyperinflation - Econlib. Retrieved 31 May 2021, from https://www.econlib.org/library/Enc/Hyperinflation.html

Venezuela

Caraballo-Arias, Y., Madrid, J., & Barrios, M. C. (2018). Working in Venezuela: how the crisis has affected the labor conditions. *Annals of global health, 84*(3), 512.

Population Pyramid of World from 1950 – 2100 (2019). *Population*

Pyramid. [Image] Retrieved from

https://www.populationpyramid.net/

Venezuela Money Supply (2021). *Trading Economics*. [Image].

Retrieved from https://tradingeconomics.com/venezuela/money-

supply-m2

Multimore, J. (2021). Reuters: Cash 'Disappearing' in Venezuela

despite Hyperinflation. *Foundation for Economic Education.*

Retrieved from https://fee.org/articles/reuters-cash-disappearing-

in-venezuela-despite-hyperinflation/

Koech, J. (2016). Oil-Rich Venezuela Tips Toward Hyperinflation.

Annual Report, Globalization and Monetary Policy Institute, 4-

11.

Pittaluga, G. B., Seghezza, E., & Morelli, P. (2021). The political

economy of hyperinflation in Venezuela. *Public Choice*, *186*(3),

337-350.

Huertas, G. (2019). Hyperinflation in Venezuela: A Stabilization

Handbook. Retrieved from

https://www.piie.com/sites/default/files/documents/pb19-13.pdf

Zimbabwe

Baldauf, S. (2008, March 25). In Zimbabwe, bread costs Z$10 million.

Retrieved from

https://www.csmonitor.com/World/Africa/2008/0325/p06s02-

woaf.html

Banque internationale pour la reconstruction et le développement.

(2008). *Migration and Remittances Factbook.* World Bank

Conkling, T. S. (2010). Analysis of the Zimbabwean Hyperinflation

Crisis: A Search for Policy Solutions (Doctoral dissertation,

Pennsylvania State University).

Coomer, J., & Gstraunthaler, T. (2011). The Hyperinflation in

Zimbabwe. *Quarterly Journal of Austrian economics*, *14*(3).

Dewa, D., Musara, E., & Mupfururi, E. (2013). Industrial decline in
Zimbabwe, Gweru post-2000: Which way now. *World Journal
of Arts, Commerce, and Sciences, 1*(1), 1-13.

Kairiza, T. (2012). *Unbundling Zimbabwe's journey to hyperinflation
and official dollarization, GRIPS Policy Information
Centre* (No. 09-12). Discussion Paper.

Matiashe, F. S. (2021, January 28). Zimbabwe: Can the central bank
hold rate as inflation soars? Retrieved from
https://www.theafricareport.com/61176/zimbabwe-can-the-
central-bank-hold-rate-as-inflation-soars/

Times, T. E. (2008, June 13). Zimbabwe inflation now over 1 million
percent. Retrieved from economictimes.indiatimes.com:
https://economictimes.indiatimes.com/news/international/zimba
bwe-inflation-now-over-1-million-per-
cent/articleshow/3126631.cms

Inflation. (2021). *Starving Billionaire*. (2016). MHSECONOMICS.

Retrieved from

https://mhseco2016.wordpress.com/2016/04/25/starving-

billionaire/

Pettinger, T. (2021). *Hyper Inflation in Zimbabwe* [Image]. Retrieved

from https://www.economicshelp.org/blog/390/inflation/hyper-

inflation-in-zimbabwe/

O'Neill, A. (2021). *Zimbabwe: Inflation rate from 1985 to*

2025 [Image]. Retrieved from

https://www.statista.com/statistics/455290/inflation-rate-in-

zimbabwe/

Mzimkhulu, L. (2019). *A Zimbabwean child carrying large currency*

bills [Image]. Retrieved from https://iharare.com/boy-carrying-

huge-amounts-of-cash-in-a-sign-of-zimbabwes-hyperinflation-

11-years-later/

Hungary

Bomberger, W. A., & Makinen, G. E. (1980). Indexation, inflationary finance, and hyperinflation: the 1945-1946 Hungarian experience. *Journal of Political Economy, 88*(3), 550-560.

Bomberger, W. A., & Makinen, G. E. (1983). The Hungarian hyperinflation and stabilization of 1945-1946. *Journal of Political Economy, 91*(5), 801-824.

Boross, E. A. (2015). The Role of the State Issuing Bank in the Course of Inflation in Hungary between 1918 and 1924. In *Die Erfahrung der Inflation im internationalen Zusammenhang und Vergleich/The Experience of Inflation International and Comparative Studies* (pp. 188-227). De Gruyter.

He, L. (2017). *Hyperinflation: A world history*. Routledge.

Kumar, V. (2015). The Hungarian Hyperinflation–A Look into the Production Side. *Studies in Applied Economics, 42*.

KUMAR, V. (2020). The Hungarian hyperinflation: A look into the production side. *Journal of Economics Library, 7*(1), 54-68.

Siklos, P. L. (1989). The end of the Hungarian hyperinflation of 1945-1946. *Journal of Money, Credit and Banking, 21*(2), 135-147.

Siklos, P. L. (Ed.). (1995). *Great inflations of the 20th century: theories, policies, and evidence.* Edward Elgar Publishing.

Valkovszky, S., & Vincze, J. (2012). Estimates of and problems with core inflation in Hungary. *Central Bank Review, 1*(1), 69-99.

Weimar Republic

Amadeo, K. (2020). Could You Survive Hyperinflation?. Retrieved 31 May 2021, from https://www.thebalance.com/what-is-hyperinflation-definition-causes-and-examples-3306097

Pettinger, T. (2021). *Hyper Inflation in Zimbabwe* [Image]. Retrieved from https://www.economicshelp.org/blog/634/economics/the-problem-with-printing-money/

Haffert, L., Redeker, N., & Rommel, T. (2019). Misremembering Weimar: Hyperinflation, the Great Depression, and German Collective Economic Memory. *Economics & Politics.*

The Weimar Republic: The Fragility of Democracy (2012). Facing

History. Retrieved from https://www.facinghistory.org/weimar-

republic-fragility-democracy/economics/inflated-weimar-

currency-1923-economics-1919-1924-inflation

Lessons from the Past - Hyperinflation in Weimar Germany (2021).

Stewart Investors. Retrieved from

https://www.stewartinvestors.com/all/insights/stap/hyperinflatio

n-in-germany.html

Salemi, M. (nd). Hyperinflation. Econlib. Retrieved from

https://www.econlib.org/library/Enc/Hyperinflation.html

Hanke, S. (2007). The World's Greatest Unreported Hyperinflation.

Cato. Retrieved from https://www.cato.org/commentary/worlds-

greatest-unreported-

hyperinflation?queryID=5d3023212546a02921dbd9abd48e1922

Goodell, N. (2018). 1920s Hyperinflation in Germany and Banknotes. Retrieved from https://www.spurlock.illinois.edu/blog/p/1920s-hyperinflation-in/283

Pardon, K. (2013). Wheelbarrows of Money. Keripardon Blog. [Image]. Retrieved from https://keripeardon.wordpress.com/2013/06/01/wheelbarrows-of-money-and-the-weimar-republic/

Hyperinflation in Weimar (n.d). Research Online. Retrieved from https://researchonline.jcu.edu.au/21599/3/21599.pdf

France

Brezis, E. S., & Crouzet, F. H. (1995). The role of Assignats during the French Revolution: an evil or a rescuer? *Journal of European economic history*, *24*(1), 7.

Trask, S. (2020). Inflation and the French Revolution: The Story of a Monetary Catastrophe. Mises Daily Articles. Retrieved from https://mises.org/library/inflation-and-french-revolution-story-monetary-catastrophe

Velde, F. R., & Weir, D. R. (1992). The financial market and government debt policy in France, 1746-1793. *Journal of Economic History*, 1-39.

France: Inflation and Revolution. (2016). American Numismatic Society. [Image]. Retrieved from http://numismatics.org/france-inflation-and-revolution/

Sargent, T. J., & Velde, F. R. (1995). Macroeconomic features of the French Revolution. *Journal of Political Economy, 103*(3), 474-518.

Ebeling, R. (2007). The Great French Inflation. Foundation of Economic Education. Retrieved from https://fee.org/articles/the-great-french-inflation/

North Korea

He, L. (2017). *Hyperinflation: A world history*. Routledge.

Powell, B. (2009). Economic 'Reform' in North Korea: Nuking the Won. *Time*. Retrieved from http://content.time.com/time/world/article/0,8599,1945251,00.html

Eberstadt, N. (2010). North Korean Money Troubles. WSJ. Retrieved from https://www.wsj.com/articles/SB10001424052748704500104574651090133811018

Hanke, S. (2013). North Korea: From Hyperinflation to Dollarization. Globe Asia. Retrieved from http://centerforfinancialstability.org/oped/NorthKoreaJuly13.pdf

Pearson, J. (2015). North Korea's Black Market Becoming the New Norm. Reuters. Retrieved from https://www.reuters.com/article/us-northkorea-change-insight-idUSKCN0SN00320151029

Yugoslavia

Cunningham, R., Desroches, B., & Santor, E. (2010). Inflation

expectations and the conduct of monetary policy: A review of

recent evidence and experience. Bank of Canada Review,

2010(Spring), 13-25.

Hanke, S. (2007). The World's Greatest Unreported Hyperinflation.

Cato. Retrieved from https://www.cato.org/commentary/worlds-

greatest-unreported-

hyperinflation?queryID=5d3023212546a02921dbd9abd48e1922

. USDCrisis. Retrieved from

He, L. (2017). Hyperinflation: A world history. Routledge.

Petrović, P., Bogetić, Ž, & Vujošević, Z. (1999). The Yugoslav

hyperinflation of 1992–1994: causes, dynamics, and money

supply process. Journal of comparative economics, 27(2), 335-353.

Stojković, M. Hyperinflation in Yugoslavia: An Example in Monetary History. Open Journal for, 43.

Taylor, A. (2012). 20 Years since the Bosnia War. The Atlantic. Retrieved from https://www.theatlantic.com/photo/2012/04/20-years-since-the-bosnian-war/100278/

Watkins, T. (2010). The Danger of printing too much Money. USDCrisis. [Image]. Retrieved from https://usdcrisis.com/history/the-danger-of-printing-too-much-money/

Ancient Rome

Andreu, J., & Blanco-Pérez, A. (2019). Signs of weakness and crisis in the Western cities of the Roman Empire (c. II–III AD). https://d1wqtxts1xzle7.cloudfront.net

Bhardwaj, D. (2020). Unit-4 Crisis of the Roman Empire. Indira Gandhi National Open University, New Delhi. http://www.egyankosh.ac.in/bitstream/123456789/67912/1/Unit-4.pdf

Butcher, K. (2015). Debasement and the decline of Rome. *Studies in ancient coinage in honor of Andrew Burnett. SPINK, London*, 181-205. https://warwick.ac.uk

Dimitrijevic, M., & Golubovic, S. (2017). Monetary System of the Ancient Rome: Implications on Contemporary Monetary Law. *Ius Romanum*, 313. https://heinonline.org

He, L. (2017). *Hyperinflation: A world history*. Routledge. https://doi.org/10.4324/9780203712061

Heather, P. J. (2018). *Rome resurgent: war and empire in the age of Justinian*. Oxford University Press. https://books.google.co.uk

Horesh, N. (2020). 2. From Coinage to Paper Money. In *Chinese Money in Global Context* (pp. 41-8 https://doi.org/10.1515/9780804788540-005

Parsons, T. (2010). *The rule of empires: those who built them, those who endured them, and why they always fall.* Oxford University Press. https://books.google.co.ke

Stange, N. (2021). Politics of Plague: Ancient Epidemics and Their Impact on Society. https://scholarship.claremont.edu/cclura_2021/4

United States

Aizenman, J., & Marion, N. (2011). Using inflation to erode the US public debt. *Journal of Macroeconomics, 33*(4), 524-541. https://doi.org/10.1016/j.jmacro.2011.09.001

Baack, B. (2008). America's first monetary policy: inflation and seigniorage during the Revolutionary War. *Financial History Review, 15*(2), 107. DOI:10.1017/S0968565008000127

Berg, E. (2021). Centralizing the Purse: Why a More Centralized National Government Was Crucial for Managing America's Revolutionary War Debt. https://digitalcommons.wku.edu/stu_hon_theses/899

Bezanson, A. (2016). *Prices and Inflation During the American Revolution, Pennsylvania, 1770-1790.* University of Pennsylvania Press. https://doi.org/10.9783/9781512814439

Bredin, D., & Fountas, S. (2018). US inflation and inflation uncertainty over 200 years. https://ruomo.lib.uom.gr

Ferraro, W. M. (2021). Washington's Revolutionary War Generals.

Hamilton, E. J. (1977). The role of war in modern inflation. *Journal of Economic History*, 13-19. https://www.jstor.org/stable/2119441

Hildebrand, D. K. (2018). The Revolutionary War and War of 1812. In *Music and War in the United States* (pp. 20-40). Routledge. ISBN 9781315194981

https://doi.org/10.1093/jahist/jaaa537

Taskinsoy, J. (2020). From Primitive Barter to Inflationary Dollar: A Warless Economic Weapon of Mass Destruction. *Available at SSRN 3542145.* https://dx.doi.org/10.2139/ssrn.3542145

China

Ebeling, R. (2014, March 21). *China's Great Inflation Helped Bring Communists to Power*. The Nassau Institute. https://www.nassauinstitute.org/article1211/

Ebeling, R. M. (2010, July 5). *The Great Chinese Inflation | Richard M. Ebeling*. Fee.org; Foundation for Economic Education. https://fee.org/articles/the-great-chinese-inflation/

Habegger, J. (1988, September). *Origins of the Chinese Hyperinflation | Jay Habegger*. Fee.org; Foundation for Economic Education. https://fee.org/articles/origins-of-the-chinese-hyperinflation/

Hewitt, M. (2007, May 22). *Hyperinflation in China, 1937 - 1949:: The Market Oracle::* www.marketoracle.co.uk. https://www.marketoracle.co.uk/Article1068.html

Inflation and CPI Consumer Price Index 1940-1949. (n.d.). InflationData.com. https://inflationdata.com/articles/inflation-consumer-price-index-decade-commentary/inflation-cpi-

consumer-price-index-1940-1949/

www.ingramcontent.com/pod-product-compliance
Lightning Source LLC
Chambersburg PA
CBHW061020220326

41597CB00016BB/1758